Soul Makeover

*Let God transform you into
the truly happy, healthy,
and fulfilled person
He created you to be*

Richard and Barbara Sheridan

New Wine Press

New Wine Press
PO Box 17
Chichester PO20 6YB
England

Unless otherwise noted, Scripture quotations are from the Amplified
Bible. Old Testament copyright © 1965, 1987 by the Zondervan
Corporation. New Testament copyright © 1954, 1958, 1987 by the
Lockman Foundation. Used by permission.

Other versions, as indicated in the text:

NIV – The Holy Bible, New International Version. Copyright © 1973,
1978, 1984 International Bible Society. Published by Hodder & Stoughton

LB – The Living Bible. Copyright © 1971. Used by permission of
Tyndale House Publishers, Inc., Wheaton, Illinois 60189. All rights
reserved.

NRSV – New Revised Standard Version Bible, Copyright © 1989,
Division of Christian Education of the National Council of the
Churches of Christ in the USA.

GN – The Holy Bible, Good News Edition. New Testament copyright ©
American Bible Society, New York 1966, 1971, and 4th edition 1976.

ISBN 1 903725 01 1

Cover by Profile Design, Chichester, West Sussex.
Typeset by CRB Associates, Reepham, Norfolk.
Printed in England by Clays Ltd, St Ives plc.

Dedication

To our parents –
Who we love
Who we know have always loved us
And done their very best for us

Acknowledgments

We would like to thank:

Those who pray regularly for us. We cherish your prayers.

Those who support us financially. You have made our continuing work, and this book, possible. Thank you for responding to God's prompting.

Those whose letters and experiences – every one precious – we have had the privilege of including in the text.
(All names have been changed to protect privacy.)

Zan, Sarah, Merle, Ed, and Clive, whose help at crucial moments encouraged us more than they can know.

Photographer Walter Dirks, Fellow of the Royal Photographic Society, for his gift of the back cover portrait.

Peter and Tim at Profile Design for their gift of the drawings.

Most of all, God the Father, Son, and Holy Spirit, who lead us into all truth, whose forgiveness covers our mistakes, and who are able to heal wounds and to restore souls.

Contents

Introduction

'A book that needs to be written'

This is essentially a book on Christian healing.

We had believed for some time that God wanted us to write it. But because there has been a tide of books on this subject in recent years, we wanted to be sure. So, we sent an outline to a best-selling Christian author.

Her reaction certainly seemed to confirm our thinking.

'It's a book that needs to be written,' she told us. 'All I can say is I wish it was published now, because I should simply love to read it, and I know it would be a great help to me in the healing ministry which God seems to be entrusting to us at the moment.'

But why is it a book that needs to be written?

The answer is that it contains priceless keys to healing and transformation of the deepest possible kind.

There will, of course, be some who have already grasped these keys, and discovered their value. But there is over-whelming evidence that, even amongst those who God is already using to heal others, such people form only a tiny minority. We are convinced that there are many more who would receive enormous benefit from knowing about the approach to healing that we have set out in this book.

I (Richard) have been ministering Christian healing, and teaching about it, full-time for more than ten years. For the last seven of these, Barbara and I have been doing this work together. In all, we have each accumulated more than two decades of experience in this area.

During this time, we have come across many (too many) people for whom the search for an answer to the seeming riddle of their own healing has been protracted, frustrating, and often desperate. We can only guess at how many have given up before finding the answers that they were seeking. But for God's kindness, we would ourselves have been among them.

We have the technology!

As a couple who have been called to give their lives to promoting and practising the supernatural healing aspects of the Gospel, we welcome the increasing range of books on this subject. We welcome, too, the many healing centres that have been opened across this needy country of ours. Our concern, however, is that these may not always approach people's healing needs as systematically or effectively as they could.

The demand for Christian healing is escalating. It is now big business in this country. Hundreds of thousands of pounds are spent every year on books, courses, and one-to-one ministry. Yet experience shows that much of this produces only a poor return. This need not be so.

Many will remember the futuristic television series of the seventies called *The Six Million Dollar Man*. The hero was an ex-air force pilot, who had been snatched from the jaws of death, and quite literally reconstructed, using high-tech engineering. Every week millions of us watched with horror as, at the beginning of each episode, a brief sequence of dramatic still frames unfolded. These recalled his terrible plane crash, and the appalling injuries that he had sustained. Our dismay turned to wonder as a steely military voice pronounced the awesome and triumphant words, 'We have the technology! We can rebuild him!'

All that was science fiction. But it is far from science fiction to say that we Christians have all that we need to be reconstructed in every way into the likeness of Christ, the perfectly whole man. We **do have** 'the technology'! And the cost need be no more than the few hours of time and effort that it takes to apply it.

It has not only been those with needs of their own that have benefited from the approach to healing which is set out in this book. Many who minister to others have also found it invaluable.

One counsellor who attended our seminars wrote:

> 'I'm sure that your model is theologically indisputable. I've been following it for the past year or eighteen months, and have found it enormously valuable ... it has worked like a dream, with marvellous results.'

Tried and tested

No book can claim to be the last word on a subject as vast as that of Christian healing. But it is our firm belief and our most sincere prayer that the pages that follow will bring invaluable equipment to the Body of Christ, both in this country and beyond.

To date, much of the written teaching that we have found to be most life-changing has been contained in weighty volumes – more suited to counsellors than to the average person. In *Soul Makeover* we have tried to distil the essence of what we have learned from such teaching to a more convenient form and size. Our aim in doing this has been to make what we have learned accessible to as wide a Christian readership as possible.

The contents of *Soul Makeover* also draw on our own direct experience of the Holy Spirit's healing work – experience gained not only in ministering to the needs of others, but also through our own continuing journeys to wholeness.

From day one of my Christian life, I (Richard) have had firsthand experience of God's miraculous healing power.

I came to know Jesus for myself when I was twenty-five, but from fourteen onwards had suffered continuously from mental and emotional difficulties, accompanied by mild depression. At times I needed medication to control this.

As I now know, all this was the result of a sequence of traumatic experiences, and of trying to run my life my own way. In particular, I gave literally my all to trying to earn the approval of human love sources.

In the months leading up to my conversion, new pressures made the depression dramatically worse. It took hold of me in such an overpowering way that I was soon brought to a complete emotional and physical standstill.

In desperation I turned to a doctor, who told me that I 'could be in and out of psychiatrists' rooms for the next ten years and still see no improvement'. Faced with this prospect, I felt any remaining enthusiasm for living begin to drain away. From then on, I was in a losing battle to find either the motivation or the physical strength to accomplish even the most basic daily routines.

Although it seemed to stretch the medical and psychological professions to their limits, my condition proved to be well within Jesus' power to heal. A concerned Christian was quick to befriend me, and to tell me about Jesus and the quality of life that He offers. It did not take me long to see that running my life my way was not working, and to ask Him to come in and be Lord instead.

No sooner had I done this than He became dramatically real to me. This changed everything. Jesus was, quite simply, powerful, unconditional love personified. Broken, unresisting, and repentant as I was, He was able to access deep places within me. The depression and its debilitating side-effects left me instantly – never to return. I did not set foot in any psychiatrist's consulting room, nor have I needed any medication since that day.

So, I have no difficulty in believing that God heals. But what I have also come to see is that the process of becoming whole needs our **active participation**. It is not simply a matter of asking God to single-handedly perform a succession of healing miracles in our lives. We have to make a series of conscious and informed choices of our own, and act on them. Unless we do, we **actually prevent** God from doing all that He can and wants to do. We deny ourselves the healing provision made available to us by His Son's crucifixion and resurrection.

It was making a choice and acting on it that made my initial healing possible. It has been some sort of choice and action that has preceded every stage of the subsequent, and in many ways more extensive, healing and transformation that I have experienced since then. The same has been true for all those to whom we have ministered.

I (Barbara) have also experienced much of God's healing.

About ten years ago I began to suffer from glandular fever and the symptoms of ME. These became progressively worse, until I was forced to stop working altogether. Further rapid decline culminated in my being taken to hospital by ambulance, so weak that I was struggling even to breathe.

For many months afterwards I was effectively an invalid, and confined to bed for much of the day. Even when I began to recover, I remained highly susceptible to infection. If there was a germ around, I not only seemed to catch it, but also to keep it for longer than anyone else. This tendency, together with the bouts of paralysing weakness characteristic of ME, persisted for several years.

Long before all this, I had become a member of the healing ministry team at my own lively and charismatic church. Here I saw a great many very caring and sincere healing prayers prayed. However, subsequent research showed that these mostly only skimmed the surface, and that any results did not last. I was aware even then of brokenness of my own stemming from childhood, and from time to time received prayer for this. But it was not really touched either.

Not until the negative experiences of my earliest years began to be 'processed' in the way that we outline in *Soul Makeover*, was God able to bring about real change in me. As this happened, the symptoms of ME disappeared.

Much of my illness was genuinely medical. But looking back I can see that continuing, unresolved hurts had an important bearing on this as well. Their weakening effect meant that I had an inbuilt susceptibility to getting ill.

When God's healing came it was an entirely supernatural thing. But what my experience taught me too was that, before we can receive this, we almost always have to do something ourselves. The good news is that there is a **comprehensive and methodical way** to find out what this is. It need not be the hit-and-miss affair that so many experience in their search for change.

In one of his best-known songs, the songwriter Keith Green, speaking for many of his generation, wrote the words: 'I want to, I need to, be more like Jesus'. That was in 1980. Shortly afterwards, while still only a young man, he was tragically killed, but the message has spread.

More recently, Kevin Prosch, another young Christian whose music reflects a spiritual hunger that is increasingly sweeping the Christian world today, recorded a song that expressed the same heartfelt sentiment. The words say:

> You could offer me things, silver lined dreams,
> But to be transformed into the image of God,
> This is what I want.
> To be drawn near, to be set free.

The central message of *Soul Makeover* is that, provided we are willing to play our part in the process, Christ-like whole-ness **really is available** to every one of us who believe. Nor is this process a complicated one.

Jesus commanded us to *'be perfect'*. Yet many Christians today assume that He was asking us to do something that is not actually possible. Certainly the journey to perfect whole-ness takes time. It has its quiet patches. But it also has its times of dramatic supernatural change. These often coincide with our greatest crises, when we can be at our most broken and receptive.

There is, of course, a vital place for reading, marking, and inwardly digesting the Word of God. But just as, at one extreme, we cannot simply expect God to change us, without any action on our part, so, at the other, we cannot in the end become like Jesus simply by learning more and more about Him in our heads, and trying harder and harder to be like Him. We need to **be changed**, and at levels of our make-up far deeper than simply that of our conscious mind.

Our aim in writing this book is to help all those who read it to make the **specific choices** that will bring about the change they are looking for in their own lives. It is our prayer that, helped by what it says, each one may be enabled to map out, and then to follow, his or her own particular route to the deep, Christ-like wholeness that is the birthright of every born-again Christian.

PART ONE

THE PROBLEM

Chapter 1

'The Bride Looks Radiant!'

'For the wedding of the Lamb has come, and His bride
has made herself ready.'
(Revelation 19:7 NIV)

Appearances can be deceptive

Barbara and I were married just seven years ago. We had both waited a long time to find the right partner, but our wedding day was well worth the wait! It was the kind that most people dream about. Down to the very last detail, everything went exactly as planned.

The ceremony itself took place in a delightful old country church. Afterwards we walked, at the head of a lively procession of our guests, down a quiet lane between green meadows, to our reception in the grounds of an elegant old stately home. There we were surrounded by loving families and friends. The summer sun shone throughout the day, as did the smiles on their faces. Everything was just perfect!

Against this background, Barbara looked radiantly happy. She felt it inside, too. But it is not like this for every bride. As Barbara's dressmaker told her, there are many whose bright smiles and immaculate looks on their big day conceal something quite different inside. Rather than expressing pure joy, they in fact hide some inner shadow.

We live in a world that concentrates increasingly on outward appearance – on making people look good. The cosmetic companies and the fashion industry, the dieticians and the workout gurus, the beauticians and, more drastically, the plastic surgeons, all queue up to offer us a better looking exterior. Together they can make a tramp look like a film star, or a grandparent look like a teenager.

Whatever they do, however, they can only change us on the outside. They may make us look better, and so distract us from other, deeper problems. But they can do nothing to bring about the more profound change that so many of us need. Despite this, the demand for what they offer is ever-increasing.

The result, worldwide, is a so-called sophisticated society, where people know more and more about how to look good, but less and less about how to truly feel it on the inside. In fact, if the kind of social problems that increasingly face our societies today are anything to judge by, the strides forward in the superficial beauty industry are more than matched by the decline in true and lasting happiness. The number of enduring, loving relationships is plummeting. At the same time, the number of violent crimes against the person is soaring – to mention just two indicators. All around us the effects of inner brokenness are evident.

God's gift to Christians

In the world, then, people may be **looking** better and better, but many are actually **feeling** worse and worse.

There can be only two reasons for this. Either people have not discovered all that life in Christ has to offer, or, if they have, they have not yet learned how to make this their own.

We Christians are different. We have done both – or have we? Are we **really** enjoying the full extent of wholeness that Christ has made available to us? Are we even sure just what is on offer?

Until now we may not have thought of it this way, but before He died, Jesus bequeathed a priceless gift to every born-again Christian: the gift of total inner radiance.

What He left us was not just a superficial shine. It was not even the kind of glow that is to be seen in the most rapturous and beautiful bride on her wedding day. Instead, it was the same perfect, deep, and enduring radiance that shone from Jesus Himself throughout His earthly life.

His gift was willed to us in a prayer.

Here is what He prayed:

> *'I pray ... for all those who will ever come to believe in Me...,* **that they all may be one***, as You, Father, are in Me and I in You,* **that they also may be one in Us***, ...*
>
> *I have given them the glory and honor which You have given Me,* **that they may be one as We are one***: I in them and You in Me, in order* **that they may become one and perfectly united***, that the world may know ... that You sent Me and that You have loved them as You have loved Me.*
>
> *Father, I desire that they ...* **may be with Me where I am***, so that they may see My glory, which You have given Me ...*
>
> *I have made* [You] *known to them ... and I will continue to make You known,* **that the love which You have bestowed upon Me may be in them** *... and that* **I may be in them***.'*   (John 17:20–26)

Jesus' prayer was a prayer for unity. He knew that only perfect unity – with God, with Him, and with one another – would guarantee us the kind of radiance that He wanted us to have.

Jesus' words make it clear that the unity He had in mind was much more than the unity of a common cause, such as the anti-abortion or anti-firearms crusades, which can unite people who might otherwise have little else in common. He was thinking of more even than the unity of having a common faith. The gift Jesus asked His Father to give each of us was that of the unity that comes from two people having a relationship so close, so empathetic, and so loving that inwardly they become one.

Complete wholeness comes from perfect, unrestricted relationship – first with God, who **is** love, and the source of

all life and health, and then with one another. Jesus knew that only relationship of this kind would provide an un-inhibited flow of the healing, resourcing Holy Spirit to our deepest places, and so produce in us the same permanent and all-pervading radiance seen in Him.

Jesus – oneness with God personified

This idea of radiance-through-unity should not surprise us. After all, Jesus' entire mission to Earth was to enable men and women to know God personally, spirit to spirit, and to love Him fully. His two great Commandments, which are familiar to all of us, could not emphasise more clearly that at the centre of life as God designed it is unreserved loving relation-ship with Him and, flowing from this, with one another.

On the cross Jesus made this possible. He provided us with all we would need, not simply to end our separation from God, but to enjoy as full a friendship with Him as Jesus Himself did while He was on Earth.

In the Gospels, Jesus shows us what having such a friend-ship with God really means. In the way He prayed, we see a man who was relaxed and familiar with God (John 17), who had total confidence in Him (Mark 14:36), and who was completely in step with Him (John 5:19–20). We see a man who knew and felt the Father's love for Him at all times. We see a man for whom the Father, despite being invisible, was as real and as tangible to Him as if He were with Him physically (John 11:42 and 16:32). We see a man who, feeling unremittingly supported, guided, loved, and em-powered by that same Father, was able to carry out (alone in every other way) the toughest life-calling ever given to a man – without flinching or faltering (Matthew 26:39).

Christians – a different reality

It has always been Jesus' intention that Christians should enjoy this same quality of relationship with Him and with His Father.

He wants us to feel constantly that we are loved and understood by Them both. He wants us to feel that we can hear from Them and speak to Them whenever we need to. He wants us to be in tune with Them, and to do the works that They are doing – empowered in the same way as He Himself was.

He prayed that we would always be so close to Him and to His Father as to be *'with* [Him]' in spirit *'where* [He is]'. He also prayed that Their love, and indeed They Themselves, would be *'in'* us. For His part, He promised that He would be *'with* [us] *always ... to the end of the world'* (Matthew 28:20 LB).

Yet, very often, this is not our experience at all. Particularly when things seem to be going badly, or our prayers do not seem to be being answered, we can see God as distant, and lose all sense of His love. Far from trusting Him, we can even blame Him for causing our woes. At times we can wonder if He is there at all.

Many books have been written on the subjects of how to pray effectively and how to hear God clearly. Some make it seem as if the business of getting through to Him, and then hearing from Him in return, is an intrinsically complex science in itself. They give the impression that it is a bit like trying to communicate with a radio station way out in space that only switches on intermittently and at random, using faulty, old-fashioned, and ill-maintained radio equipment. To get through is an achievement, but to receive and understand a message is near miraculous. It requires years of patience, and, even then, what we hear seems to have to be carefully confirmed!

More questions than answers

Why is this so? Why is relationship with God so often viewed in these and other ways that are so far from what Jesus Himself experienced, and envisaged for us?

Why do so many Christians not describe their relationship with God as something that always comes naturally and feels good – that is real, reliable, and empowering on a daily basis? Why do we not feel all the time as if the most wonderful, loving, and powerful Person we could ever imagine were with us – almost as if He were here in the flesh, like a natural parent, brother, sister, marriage partner or friend? Why are God the Father and Jesus, for so many of us, like that radio station way out in space? We know that They are there, if only because we have heard from Them in the past, but They often seem far away and almost impossible to contact in the present. And why do we feel this way despite, sometimes, having taken in many hours of teaching to the contrary?

It was second nature to Jesus that God the Father was always there – full of love, understanding, and the power to do anything that He asked. He never doubted that God was both perfect and perfectly in tune with Him. For Jesus, His Father was truly the God of Psalm 139. He was a Father who knew at all times where His Son was, and exactly what He was doing and thinking. He was a Father who was always there thinking fond and proud thoughts of Him, and acting to protect Him. He was, quite simply, the Father to end all fathers.

Far from being second nature to many of us, it is often only by continued conscious effort that we can even begin to exercise and experience the various facets of Jesus' relationship with God in our own relationship with both Him and His Father. Why is this?

Christ's earthly life experience was one of closeness to the Father, of being fully in tune with Him, and of maintaining a perpetual and unbroken heart-love flow between Himself and God. Because of this He was able at all times to feel positive, loving, confident, and secure. Why does it often seem to be so different for us?

Why is our Christian walk, as Paul himself acknowledges in Chapter 7 of Romans, persistently dogged by powerful inner currents that pull us off course? Why do so many of the things that came naturally to Jesus require at best a conscious effort on our part, or, at worst, elude us completely? Why are deeply rooted feelings of heaviness or isolation or fear or captivity, which rob us of radiance, as familiar to us as feelings of lightness or lovedness or security or freedom?

Why does God, though unquestionably real to us in some ways, often **seem** distant and small, and hard to 'contact' and to draw upon for new strength? And why, as a consequence, is it often people, who seem that much more real and present, and what **they** think about us or do to us, that routinely dictate how we feel, rather than the reality of God and all that He is?

Why, too, do so many of us experience so much ill-health?

Daring to believe

Faced with Scripture on the one hand, but a barrage of questions like these on the other, many of us have had to grapple with one overriding question: can we really ever expect to become like Jesus the man?

In the Introduction, I (Richard) described how the immediate impact of Jesus on my life was to bring sudden and sweeping change, wonderfully and miraculously healing me of depression. Light invaded darkness, and hope invaded despair. The need to struggle to earn love was swept away by a love that demanded nothing of me, and grinding aimlessness gave way to a new and exciting purpose – that of gratefully and enthusiastically following Jesus and doing my best for Him. And yet, as time passed and the initial euphoria settled, it became clear that **not everything** had changed.

Paradoxical as it may seem, it has been the things that Jesus' supernatural presence and power did **not** immediately change that have led to the writing of this book.

Although my conversion experience had undoubtedly been a momentous one, I became increasingly aware that I had not, in some indefinable way, taken possession of my full inheritance as a child of God.

When Jesus had first begun to woo me into repentance and a living relationship with Him, He had made a statement, through the pages of the Bible, that had struck me above all

others. He had said, *'I have come ... that you might have life ...
in all its fullness'* (John 10:10 GN), or, as I received it, 'I have
come so that you can start to **really live**.'

I had come into relationship with Love and Truth Himself.
This had brought about miraculous and dramatic inner
change. I was in contact with the most wonderful and
powerful Person we could ever hope to meet and to enjoy
friendship with. Yet, as time went on, I became conscious of
many ways in which my thinking and my feelings, as well as
the lifestyle and actions that flowed from them, were not
fully what one would expect to come from this.

It amounted to this: although I had been wonderfully and
supernaturally freed from being gripped to the point of
paralysis by a sense of isolation, anxiety, aimlessness, and
hopelessness (the key ingredients of my depression), those
old hounds were still about. I was in a relationship with Love
Himself, and yet still often **felt alone**; with Peace Himself,
and yet often **felt worried**; with Joy Himself, and yet often
felt heavy; with the Way Himself, and yet often **felt at a loss**
to know precisely where to go next; and with the Ultimate
Evangelist Himself, and yet still **finding it a struggle** to
produce even a meagre harvest in terms of lives brought
to Him.

Something inside me – even if it was only an instinct that
Jesus would not make promises that **He** could not keep –
seemed to be telling me that my relationship with God
through Jesus was not having anything like the impact on
me that God intended.

I have since discovered not only that I was right, but also
that this has been the experience of countless other Christians. We have come into what is **potentially** a full
relationship with God and full Christ-likeness of character,
health, lifestyle, and experience, but **reality** has been something quite different. It is as if a connection has been made,
and yet has proved, if we are honest, flawed and faulty
compared with the connection that existed between Jesus
the man and His (and our) Heavenly Father. We have sensed
that we are missing out, but wondered whether there was

anything we could do but accept this as a permanent, unavoidable consequence of our fallen nature.

Some twenty years now of life-changing journeying with Jesus, have led both Barbara and I to the conviction that forms the basis of this book. It is founded on the Bible and backed up by experience – our own, and that of many others known to us personally. It is the conviction that the answer to the question 'Can we ever really expect to become like Jesus the man?' is: 'Yes. Just like Him.' Not only do we believe that we can and should, for our part, expect to become like Him, we also believe that this is what Jesus Himself wants for us.

We are in good company in believing this. The great St Paul himself believed it too. He wrote that his own greatest goal in life was *'to know Christ'* and to become *'like Him'* (Philippians 3:10 NIV). In language echoed by St John in Revelation, he likened the oneness and intimacy that God wants with us, through Jesus, to that of a marriage relationship.

In Ephesians 5:25–27 he wrote that *'...Christ loved the church and gave himself up for her to make her holy, cleansing her by the washing of water through the word, and to present her to himself as a **radiant** church* [a bride], *without stain or wrinkle or any other blemish, but holy and blameless'* (NIV – parenthesis ours).

Jesus sees us as His bride. He wants us to be whole and to enjoy full loving relationship with God and with our earthly brothers and sisters, **just as He did as a man**. Only then will we be a bride who is radiant through and through.

This is a truth that every member of the Body of Christ should know. [Though for ourselves, as for those whose walk toward Christ-likeness we have shared, we would hasten to add, like Paul, that it is *'not that* [we] *have already ... been made perfect, but* [we] *press on to take hold of that for which Christ Jesus took hold of* [us]*'* (Philippians 3:12 NIV).]

Jesus is not like a politician who, before an election, makes attractive promises but cannot always deliver. He is Truth and the Son of God, who **can** deliver. It is His longing that we should **experience for ourselves** the 'radiance-through-relationship' that we have described. His life, death, and resurrection have provided us with all that we need to **actually do this**.

Entering the 'Promised Land'

Our primary purpose in what follows is to enable our readers to make full use of this provision, and so to become fully the people God meant each one of us to be. We will start by examining the differences between Jesus' inner make-up and our own. This look under Jesus' 'skin' will explain the quality of His relationships and life, as against ours. It will also show us why the differences need not be permanent, and why fundamental change is possible. Finally we will look at how we can set about actually experiencing this.

Diana came on one of our regular Courses. In these we first teach essentially what is written in the pages that now follow. We then allow time for people to put what they learn into practice, so that they can experience the healing work of the Holy Spirit for themselves.

Diana had been a Christian for many years, but after the Course had this to say:

> 'The last few weeks have been like starting afresh. I have felt a new positiveness ... and bags of energy. I have not been able to stop praising God. Suddenly, being me is no longer the drag that it used to be. On the last night I felt so confident of God's love, I was left wondering if my faith had been real 'til then! The good news is that these feelings continue!'

In the pages that follow, we shall be explaining what for Diana, and for many others, has proved to be a clear and motivating path of choice and action, and has led them to radically greater Christ-likeness. Our aim in this book is to enable those who read it to make the choices that will open the door to supernatural change in their lives. It is to enable them to **actually become** more like Christ, **who was healthy in every way**; to experience **a new closeness to God, and a new wholeness.**

If you are aware that the full life and the radiance that Jesus came to give you are not yet yours; if you are not satisfied with being told that your salvation was complete in all senses at conversion, or that your fallen nature means that you can never expect to change significantly; if you believe that things would be different if, rather than continually trying to be and to do what you have been 'taught', you could have your deep internal furniture permanently rearranged into a more Christ-shaped configuration; and, if you are prepared to play your part – it might just be that what we have to say in the pages that follow is tailor-made for you.

May you hear God's voice as you read on. May He work in you, and bless and **change** you, so that you too can experience your own 'soul makeover'.

Chapter 2

Made in Heaven

*'In the beginning [before all time] was the Word [Christ],
and the Word was **with God** ...
He was present originally with God.'*
(John 1:1–2)

*'God said, "**Let Us** [Father, Son, and Holy Spirit] make
mankind in **Our** image, after **Our** likeness ... '*
(Genesis 1:26)

The ways in which we fall short of Christ's perfection are
not merely superficial. They go to our very roots.

What we teach in this book has the potential to make a
person completely new. This will affect every area of our lives
– the way we think, the way we feel, and our physical health.
The process is not complicated, but it will not make sense
unless we first have a basic appreciation of the way we
human beings are put together by God, and of the way He
intends us to develop as people – from conception to fully
mature adulthood. We start here.

Human beings – the main components

We are each made up of a body, a spirit, and a soul.

Our bodies are the physical home in which our spirits and
souls live .

Our bodies change. As we feed them with physical food, they both grow and alter shape. Then, eventually, they age and die.

Our spirits are the essence of who we are. They express themselves through our bodies. They are also the life-force behind those bodies (Figure 1).

Figure 1

Unlike our bodies, our spirits do not change or degenerate during the course of our lives. They have a self-contained completeness, which they keep – although they can be positively or negatively influenced or controlled from outside themselves. When our bodies become too old, infirm, or damaged to be sustained any longer, our spirits simply leave them and return to God.

Figure 1 shows our spirits as if they were entirely confined within our bodies. They **are** firmly embedded and anchored inside us, but at the same time they project what we are **beyond** our physical frames.

As a little boy growing up in the Far East, I (Richard) was fascinated by the fireflies that visited our garden at night. These little creatures are like tiny flying lighthouses. From the same built-in power source that keeps them alive, they are able to generate and to flash their own bright beams of light far out into the surrounding darkness.

We are like them. Our spirits are the resident power source that sustains our lives. But, like those beams of light from a firefly, they too can radiate out from inside us – shining out through our physical bodies (Figure 2).

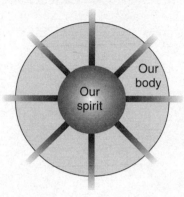

Figure 2

As the very essence of each of us, our spirits project something far more wonderful than just rays of light or waves of energy. They project the very people that we are to the world around us (Figure 3).

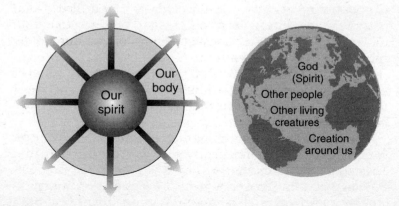

Figure 3

As well as exuding the essence of who we are, our spirits also experience our surroundings for themselves. Through their own sensitivity, and through the 'stethoscope' of our physical senses (sight, hearing, smell, touch, and taste), like radar, they gauge ultra-sensitively whatever we encounter. As this happens, we relate fully to the world around us, and truly 'taste' all of life's rich and varied flavours (Figure 4).

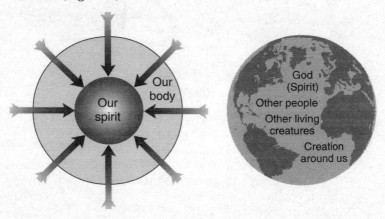

Figure 4

Our spirits are thus in a continuous dialogue with the world around us. They make us known to that world, and they experience it (Figure 5).

(In our materialistic society, we are constantly under pressure to focus our attention on physically visible things. In a multitude of different ways, emphasis is placed on what can be seen and touched. Because of this, it is easy to forget the crucial part that our spirits play in making us the people we are, and in our proper enjoyment of life.)

Once God has placed a spirit in our bodies, we exist as people, and can experience and interact with all that is around us. We can begin to enjoy God's Creation.

However, this is not enough for us. We are not content to simply live in a series of random sensations. A part of us has a pre-programmed purpose. That part is our soul.

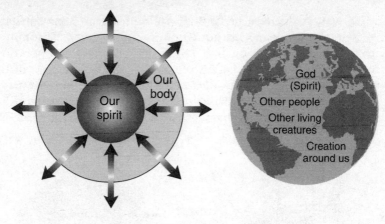

Figure 5

The soul

Every human soul has a built-in, threefold agenda. It wants to love and be loved, to learn, and to fulfil its own unique life-calling. Further, it is designed to crave that very nourishment that will enable it to fulfil all of these ambitions: God's truth-bearing love.

Only God, who is love, can satisfy all our soul's desires, and enable us to fulfil our destiny. This is why the Psalmist says:

> '*As the hart pants and longs for the water brooks, so I pant and long for You, O God. My inner self thirsts for God, for the living God ... For He satisfies the longing soul and fills the hungry soul with good.*' (Psalm 42:1–2 & 107:9)

The soul not only craves God's love and truth. Once it receives them, it can also retain them. As our spirit dialogues with our surroundings, our soul draws off what it is looking for and salts it away. This both satisfies our emotional needs and enables us to grow.

The soul and the spirit are partners, each with its own particular speciality.

We see the soul as being like a bubble of gossamer-fine gauze that completely surrounds our spirit within us. It's fine mesh ensures that in itself it causes no obstruction or dampening of the spirit's dialogue with the outside world. This is important, because the spirit is our point of contact with God and the outside world. It is vital that it is given unhindered freedom to dialogue with them both (Figure 6).

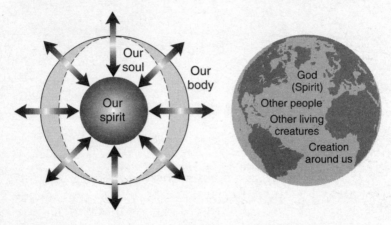

Figure 6

Moment by moment, as we live, the spirit communes with God and with His creation, and projects its experiences in full colour into the soul. As a mirror deflects beams of light, so our spirits deflect an image of all that they encounter towards our souls (Figure 7).

The soul gratefully receives the experiences of God's world that the spirit projects into its retentive pores. It is as if, from the moment we are given life, a super-sophisticated video camera is set running. This permanently registers every detail that comes home to our spirits, throughout our lives. This includes not only what we see and hear, but the accompanying feelings and sensations as well.

Having recorded our experiences through the faculty of our memories, the soul subjects these to the processing of the mind. The mind draws conclusions from them, and stores

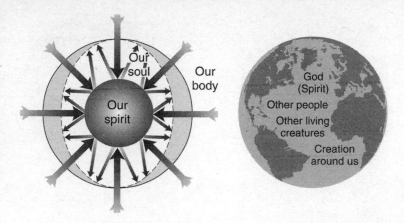

Figure 7

these in the soul to make up an ever more comprehensive overview of how life works, and how it should be navigated. We thus acquire our own, unique, personalised, built-in encyclopaedia for living.

The spirit is naturally spontaneous and impulsive, whilst the soul grows wise by experience. It tempers and channels the spirit's spontaneity with this wisdom.

Furthermore, while simple memory holds its information merely passively, giving us the option of referring to it if we wish, the soul actively thrusts what it contains at the spirit. In the same way that one person can be a constant companion and adviser to another, so our soul acts as a constant companion and adviser to our spirits.

Our souls learn everything that they know through our spirits. However, once they have been given information and drawn their conlusions from it, they constantly and actively thrust these back at those same spirits. Their 'knowledge' becomes authoritative advice on how life works, and on how our spirits should behave in different circumstances. They give this advice whether they are specifically asked for it or not. They become the guardians and perpetuators of a particular view of life, and how it should be lived (Figure 8).

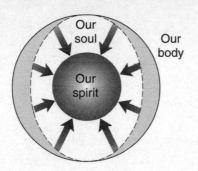 

Figure 8

The mechanism of our souls enables us to retain our experiences, and to build them into a coherent worldview. In doing this it enables us to learn, to grow, and to mature. Without the ability that we have to 'build' a soul, our spirits would live perpetually and only in the present moment. The lessons of each day would slip through our hands like mercury. But whilst our souls make life an increasingly rich experience, they mean, too, that **we are inwardly shaped by past experience**. In living under the influence of our souls, our spirits are to a large extent controlled by our past, which moulds our soul's outlook on life.

It could be said that we live in two worlds at the same time. One is the real world around us. The other is the inner world of our soul. With its God-given drives and its accumulated worldview and strategy for living, this also surrounds our spirits.

There is another aspect to our souls that is important to grasp if we are to understand our inner construction, how we behave, and why only God's power can transform us into the likeness of Jesus. This is that **they store information chronologically in layers**.

The earliest information that our spirits gather and store, and the conclusions we draw from this, are held at the deepest level of our souls. Subsequent information is laid over this, at shallower levels (Figure 9).

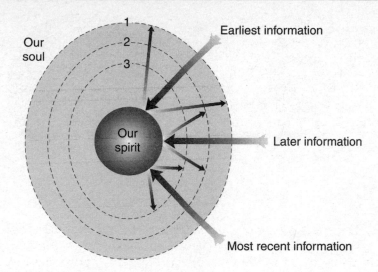

Figure 9

The experiences and world-view contained in the deepest layers of our souls (1) is the bedrock on which the later layers (2, 3 etc.) are built. This means that our earliest experiences not only affect how we think and behave as people from then on, but also all our subsequent soul-building. They thus go into deciding how we meet and incorporate later experiences into our souls.

In terms of our fundamental make-up, then, the earlier an experience the more profound and lasting its effects on our soul will be. Later experiences do have an impact, but they never of themselves eradicate the effect of earlier ones. As we shall see, only God can do that.

The deepest layers of our souls are often referred to as our subconscious. Throughout our lives the subconscious continues to project its contents at our spirits (Figure 10). It influences the way we think and act, but its detailed content becomes invisible to us. For example, others may describe us as happy or sad souls, as trusting or suspicious souls, as kind or cruel souls, without our being able to recall precisely the experiences and conclusions that have made us that way. In

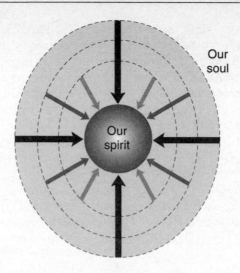

Figure 10

this sense, much of our thinking and behaviour is now driven by forces beyond our conscious control.

It has been said by psychologists that the way we react to situations is 10% to do with what is happening in the present, and 90% to do with what has happened to us in the past. Such things cannot, of course, be measured in numbers. But what this underlines is that we are only consciously in charge of a small fraction of what we think and do. The rest is running on autopilot, on a course which, if we are adults, was locked in many years, if not decades, ago.

Summarising the soul

The soul is a God-given facility that gives us basic appetites, and a direction for our lives. It also enables us to draw off and retain information and conclusions of all kinds about the world that our spirits encounter. What accumulates there becomes an encyclopaedia of information about all aspects of life, which we carry around inside us. This encylopaedia, built up over time, includes each individual's personal, detailed guide to the business of living. Our soul constitutes an inner world of information in which our spirit lives. Taking account of the facts of life, as it sees them, it constantly steers our spirit's activity, with the ultimate aim of meeting its inbuilt desires and goals in life – most importantly to feel loved.

Our spirits, which are us, live in two worlds at the same time. They live within the physical world that surrounds us. But they also live within the inner world of our souls. The first consists of beings and objects – what they are and what they do – over which we have little or no control. The second consists of a view of the world which is entirely self-made.

Developing a perfect soul

We have described the different parts of the equipment that we are given at birth, and how they work. But what is perfect maturity? And how do we get there?

Perfect maturity means having a soul that enables us (i.e. our spirits) both to be ourselves, and to have empathetic, and unhindered relationship with God, other people, and the Creation.

Such a soul will be one that has at its centre a clear picture of God – that is, of His nature, and of His centrality to and sovereignty over everything in the known universe. It will also carry God's perspective on the Creation and how a person should live within it – God's values, if you like.

Building a soul like this means having God's truth-bearing presence constantly with us. It requires accurate and complete information on all aspects of the world around us, as He sees it, to be available to us throughout our formative years. It also requires a spirit that is perfectly attuned and unreservedly receptive to God, and so able to accept this information fully.

Since the Fall, these conditions have not existed in the life of any individual – with one exception.

Jesus' perfect soul

We have seen that our souls are like constant advisers to
our spirits. A perfectly constructed soul would ensure that
a person's spirit experienced and responded to life as
God intended – in other words, that it lived life to the
full, and without sinning. Above all, it would enable that
spirit to have truly empathetic relationship with others.
It would direct and guide that spirit to automatic Christ-
likeness.

Jesus' soul was the only perfectly constructed soul that this
world has ever seen. He is the only human being who has
ever had the capacity to enjoy full, perfect, continuing, and
unimpaired relationship with God, and with the world
around Him.

Jesus – wholly receptive spirit meets perfect
nurturing environment

The Bible makes only scant reference to the process of Jesus'
inner development from crib to adulthood. The New Testament bears out the classic theologians' assertion that He was
'fully God', but 'fully man' at the same time. From this it
seems fair to assume that, during His earthly life, He was
confined within the same biological and spiritual equipment
as we are. As well as being told that in Jesus the Word *'became
flesh'* (John 1:14), we are also told that from birth He
'grew and became strong in spirit, filled with wisdom' (Luke
2:40). There is also a reference in Hebrews to His **learning**
(Hebrews 5:8, 9).

These pieces of the jigsaw give a picture of Jesus under-
going the same process of growth to adult maturity as we do.
This process, which we will be describing more fully in the
pages that follow, is essentially one of absorbing from the
environment around us various key elements of a food for
nurture, which God has designed for this purpose. As we will
see in the next chapter, in our fallen world that food for
nurture has become contaminated by sin. Absorbing this

contaminated diet into our souls is one of the main reasons that we all grow up damaged.

We have headed this section, 'Jesus – wholly receptive spirit meets perfect nurturing environment'. A receptive spirit is one that is in permanent, full communion with God. It is one that is completely open to the good things that He sends. Such was Jesus' spirit. And it was because He had absorbed all that God wanted Him to by way of nurture, without any contamination, that He grew up to be the perfect man that He was.

However, given that He grew up here on Earth, within a sinful family, how was this possible?

Once again, the Bible does not enable us to give a definite answer. So some speculation is inevitable. But here are three possibilities.

The first is that, although the child Jesus was physically situated on Earth, by the power of His presence and Spirit God somehow surrounded Him with Himself. In this way, He could have ensured that, during His soul-building, Jesus received perfect food for nurture, and was prevented from absorbing any earthly contaminants.

The second possibility is that Jesus' own spirit was the key to His perfect soul-building. This may have enabled Him to commune with God in heaven at all times, and to receive perfect food for nurture direct from Him. God's presence and power flowing to Him in this way may have enabled Him also to repel impurities from the world around Him.

Both of these sets of conditions would have enabled Jesus to build, from scratch, a perfect soul in which to live the sinless earthly life that He did.

The third possibility is that, unlike us, Jesus did not begin His soul-building from scratch (beginning at the moment He was conceived in Mary's womb), but instead brought an already formed soul into this world with Him. This possibility might explain Jesus' sense of the continuity of His existence as the Word, who, having come from the Father's side to Earth, was destined to return there.

A person's entire life history is carried in their soul. This includes the record of where they were born and grew up; who they were born to; the people they have known; where they have been; what they have achieved; and how others have classified them by their words and actions. These all contribute to their sense of who they are.

Through most of His earthly life Jesus preferred to leave it to people to work out His identity for themselves. We hear Him asking His disciples: *'Have I been with all of you for so long a time, and do you not recognise and know Me yet?'* (John 14:9). And again, *'Who do you say I am?'* (Luke 9:20). John tells us that He was *'full of grace and truth'* (John 1:14). For those with eyes to see, what He was like spoke more than adequately of who He was.

Towards the end, however, He came under direct pressure from both His disciples and His inquisitors to explain who He was. His answers may have reflected the historical record in a soul already filled and formed before His earthly birth:

> *'...I know where I came from and where I am going ... I came from the Father and entered the world; now I am leaving the world and going back to the Father ... You are right in saying I am a King ... My kingdom is not of this world. In fact, for this reason I was born, and for this I came into the world, to testify to the truth.'*
>
> (John 8:14; 16:28; 18:36–37 NIV)

The Bible tells us that Jesus, the Word, was *'with God ... in the beginning'*. It also says that everything that has been created was created through Him (John 1:1–3). So, Jesus' relationship with God goes back even before Creation – to eternity.

It is possible that the effect of the length and quality of His relationship with the perfect Father was that, by the time Jesus became confined in a human body, His soul had long since been fundamentally formed. It is possible that God's plan, that *'all the divine fullness – the sum total of the divine perfection, powers, and attributes – should dwell in*

Him permanently' (Colossians 1:19), was a *fait accompli* – completed long before Jesus entered the world as a man.

If this were so, then in Jesus the pot that contains a person's character may already have been filled to the brim with the essence of God, leaving no room for anything else. It might explain why Paul wrote,

> *'For in Him the whole fullness of Deity (the Godhead) continues to dwell in bodily form – giving complete expression of the divine nature ...* [and making Him] *the exact likeness of the unseen God.'* (Colossians 2:9 & 1:15)

It would be as if He had been 'brought up' personally and exclusively by the One who is perfectly and limitlessly loving, empathetic, intelligent, knowledgeable, wise, and strong, and had then spent countless years in fellowship with Him.

Compared to this, His thirty-three years in the fallen environment of this world would have been briefer than the blink of an eye. It would have had no formative effect whatsoever on the perfect encyclopaedia and plan for living that His soul already housed.

According to this scenario, Jesus' time on earth would not have been formative. It would have played no part in making Him the perfect person we see in the pages of the Bible. Spending time on this Earth, being Himself, and interacting with its sinful inhabitants from within the confines of a human body, may have been a new experience for the unchanging Word of God. But only in this sense could He have been said to have 'learned' or 'grown' as a result of it.

We can never know for sure precisely how God contrived to bring about Jesus' perfection as a human being. There is no scenario that can be proven beyond doubt, though many learned theologians have pondered the exact nature of Christ's humanity down the ages. In the end we must accept this as an area in which, beyond the written Word and our own powers of reason and understanding, we need the

Spirit's revelation. Even then we may not be given to understand it fully.

The record of Jesus' life in the New Testament was clearly
intended to provide us with a model of human perfection for
our own lives. Jesus Himself told us to copy this. He said:

> *'You, therefore, must be perfect, as your heavenly Father is*
> *perfect [that is, grow into complete maturity of godliness in*
> *mind and character ...]'*   (Matthew 5:48)

In Ephesians, Paul underlines to us that it is God's intention
that we should become perfect. This, he tells us means
becoming *'wholly filled and flooded with God Himself'* (Ephesians 3:19). In view of this it would be tragic if we were just to
dismiss Jesus as being a special case – simply another species
from ourselves, and so to abandon all real aspiration to
become like Him.

Jesus **was** fully human. He was perfect. In His written
Word, God calls us to be just like Him. He tells us also that He
has provided *'everything we need'* (2 Peter 1:3 LB) to make this
possible.

Most Christians believe that it is the **differences** between
us that are fundamental. In fact it is the **similarities** that are
fundamental. Understanding this will help us greatly in our
quest for wholeness.

The perfect soul in action

Jesus described Himself as *'the Truth'* (John 14:6). He could
have said, 'I speak the truth.' But He went further. It was as if
He was saying: 'My soul is so completely impregnated with
the truth – which has the existence, the supremacy, and the
ways of God at its centre – that I actually AM the truth. The
truth and I are inseparable. I carry nothing but the truth, so
nothing but truth comes out from me.'

We cannot know exactly what it was like to be the spirit that
lived in Jesus' soul, but we can make some deductions from
His words and behaviour as they are described in the Bible.

A well-known episode from Jesus' childhood illustrates the pre-eminent place in His soul of God, and of God's perspective on life.

At the age of twelve, we are told in Luke's gospel, Jesus goes up to Jerusalem with His parents and others to celebrate the Feast of the Passover. When it is over, His parents set off on the journey home, mistakenly assuming that Jesus is travelling with other friends in their group. Having walked for a day without seeing Him, they begin to look for Him amongst their travelling companions. Searching high and low, and yet failing to find Him, they return to Jerusalem.

It is several days before they finally track Him down in the Temple, where He is discussing deep questions about God with the Jewish religious teachers. The upshot is that Jesus is confronted by two extremely anxious and exasperated parents, who immediately begin to take their son to task for what they see as His thoughtless and irresponsible behaviour.

Far from accepting their rebuke, Jesus counters with a question of His own. What He asks them amounts to this: 'Why all the searching? Knowing me as you do, could you not have worked out where I would be and what I would be doing?' (See Luke 2:41–52.)

Two aspects of this account of Jesus as a boy illustrate the difference between Him and other people. These are His astounding knowledge of things to do with God, and His complete lack of any need to please people.

The Temple school, where Jesus was engaged in discussion, was famous throughout Judea. At a time like the Passover, the leading Jewish rabbis would gather there to discuss and to teach important truths about God. Yet this particular twelve year-old's in-depth knowledge and understanding on this subject were such as to 'astonish' even men of their calibre. The more we think about this, the more it highlights just how saturated with truth about God His soul must have been.

In Jesus' reaction to His parents' attack, we get still more insight into the content of His soul. To a level deeper even than that of His allegiance to His parents, Jesus was loyal to

God. He not only instinctively knew God's will, but also
saw everything else as secondary to obeying and pleasing
Him (Luke 2:49). Only a heavenly grounding could have
produced such an overwhelming sense of security in God's
love, and such a clear-sighted and firm allegiance to His
agenda.

Pervading Jesus' soul were two unshakeable pieces of
information: He knew that the God who *'is love'* (1 John
4:16) unreservedly loved and supported Him. He also knew
what that God would do in every situation. This undergirded
all His spirit's thinking and acting. This soul-knowledge
caused Him, for example, to continue to love in the face of
all that His torturers and executioners did to Him.

One result of Jesus' long and close relationship with
God the Father was that an unwavering trust in Him was
written into His soul. For Jesus it was incontrovertible fact
that God existed and was completely in control of events
on this Earth. We are wrong if for one moment we think
that Jesus' sweat (*'like drops of blood'*) in the Garden of
Gethsemane had anything to do with doubts about whether
God was there, in control, or knew what He was doing.
It is inconceivable that such doubts should have had any
place in Him. What this showed was simply that He was an
acutely intelligent human being, who was sharply able to
picture the physical, emotional, and spiritual torture that lay
ahead.

It is often when a person is under the severest pressure that
we come to see what really lies at the foundations of their
make-up. No pressure could be greater than the immediate
threat of crucifixion and death that Jesus faced after His
capture by the Jewish authorities. As He was 'squeezed' by
one torture and interrogation after another, what ruled His
reactions was this same picture of a God who is pivotal to this
world, and who is completely in control in all the events that
take place in it.

When Pilate threatened Jesus with his own supposed power
over Him, Jesus' reply emphatically revealed the content of
His soul:

'You would have no power at all over me unless it were given to you from above.' (John 19:11 LB)

Jesus was quite different from everyone else that has ever lived. His wholly receptive spirit, together with the perfectly pure food for nurture that He received from the Father, resulted in a perfect soul. In this sense, He was made in heaven.

Chapter 3

Made on Earth

'Surely I was sinful at birth,
*sinful **from the time my mother conceived me**.'*
(Psalm 51:5 NIV)

*'For it is **from within** ... that evil intentions come: fornication,*
theft, murder, adultery, avarice, wickedness, deceit,
licentiousness, envy, slander, pride, folly. All these evil things
***come from within** and they defile a person.'*
(Mark 7:21–23 NRSV)

'It seems to be a fact of life that, when I want to do what is
right, I inevitably do what is wrong. I love to do God's will so
*far as my new nature is concerned; but there is **something else***
***deep within me**, in my lower nature, that is at war with my*
*mind and wins the fight and makes me a slave to **the sin that***
***is still within me**. In my mind I want to be God's willing*
*servant, but instead I find myself **still enslaved to sin**.'*
(Romans 7:21–23 LB)

Our soul-building is different from Jesus' in two crucial
ways.

First, we begin life with our spirits separated from God.
Second, the environment around us, and which we absorb
into our souls, is polluted with sin.

Rebellious spirit meets imperfect world

It was God's original design that we human beings should be brought up, and do our soul-building, united with Him in spirit, and in an atmosphere of perfect love, truth, and sinlessness.

We **could** have experienced this. When our first ancestors, Adam and Eve, were placed down here on Earth, they enjoyed God's full presence, as He 'walked' an unspoilt world with them. However, they were seduced by the Devil and disobeyed God. Their choice introduced sin into our environment, and caused our sinless God to withdraw His presence. That sin, incubating and multiplying in generations of men and women since then, has become a barrier that has cut every one of us off from a full experience of God's presence, and has devastated the environment in which we grow up.

We all inherit our forbears' fallen nature, and are born as sinners. We are all also born into a world where God and what He is like are significantly obscured, and where the environment that He created for our development is infected by the ways of sinful people, and by the Devil.

It is this atmosphere, rather than the one God intended, that our delicate and sensitive spirits encounter from conception. Here, in separation from God, and in varying degrees of ignorance, we set about building a soul for our spirits to live in. The result is that Christ-likeness **mixed with imperfection** is woven into our deepest fabric.

How God's best for human development goes wrong

As we have seen, we all receive our basic components at conception. What follows is simply an inner (soul) and an outer (physical) journey to full maturity. We complete this successfully only if:

1. the food for growth (both spiritual and physical) that God has prescribed is available to us, and
2. we actually take all of this in.

Although we are making this distinction between our souls and our bodies, it is important to be clear that the proper development and the health of both are vitally linked. We all understand that a poor physical condition can affect the way we feel inside. But what is much less well known is just how much the condition of our souls affects our bodies. This means that **the food that feeds our souls is ultimately every bit as important to our physical health as what we eat and drink**.

We say again, the food that feeds our souls is **truth-bearing love**.

God is the ultimate source of all love, but He has decided to allow human agents to be partners with Him in the task of feeding young souls, and bringing them to maturity. **In both cases, relationships are the channels through which this soul-food flows**.

In Chapter 7 we shall be looking in detail at the ingredients of truth-bearing love. We shall also be looking at what God's chosen agents have to do if they are to work with Him in feeding this into our souls. If this soul-food is to do its work, however, it must not only be made available to us. We must also be fully open to receiving it. If we are in any way unreceptive or closed to God or His human agents, then our souls suffer.

Everyone begins life with some resistance to the things of God. And life in this world always increases this. Adam and Eve's Fall has meant that from the start we are separated from God in spirit. We are self-centred and tend to go our own way, rather than God's. On top of this, we all experience imperfect love. We receive this into our souls in ways that further damage our ability to relate to, and receive from, both God and His human agents.

The most important people with whom God chooses to share the creative process, and to whom He gives the responsibility of administering much of His truth-bearing love, are our parents. But other relatives, friends, teachers, and indeed all those with whom we have contact as we are growing up, also have a part to play.

We can illustrate God's recipe for our inner development by means of a diagram (Figure 11).

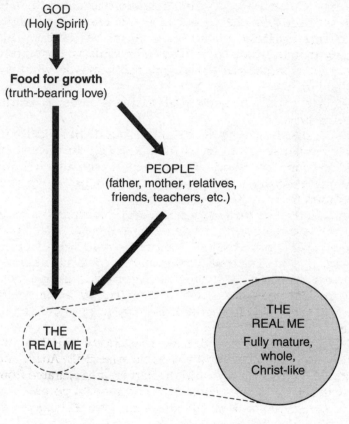

Figure 11

This diagram represents the ideal situation. Here all the relationships that are channels of nourishment are in place. The soul has the right diet available to it, and the spirit is completely receptive.

However, what we **actually** experience falls short of this ideal. From the outset, two factors detract from this process.

Firstly, there is the un-Christ-likeness, and therefore the shortcomings as nurturers, of God's chosen human agents (Figure 12).

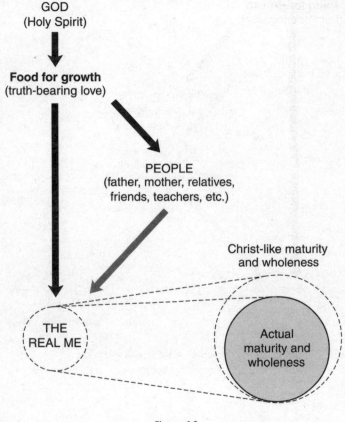

Figure 12

Added to the imperfection of human agents, there is the natural rebelliousness of our own spirits. In addition, as time goes by, our increasingly malformed souls make us less and less receptive to God and to His human channels of nurture (Figure 13).

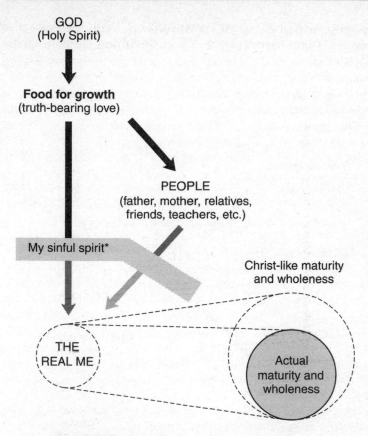

Figure 13

Imperfect souls

The most damaging thing that God's human agents do is to feed our souls with an inaccurate and incomplete picture of God, and of how He wants our lives lived. They veil Him from our sight, so that we do not fully understand what He is like – His character, His power, and the quality of His love for us. Rather than seeing Him as He is, we actually perceive Him as being like them. They also veil His recipe for living from us, so that in many respects we absorb wrong ways of living life. **Our** souls' view of the way life works is centred on people and their ways, rather than on God and His nature. As a result, we copy them, and grow up doing a mixture of what seems convenient in the short term and what is right by God, and so reaps true, enduring blessing.

We **all** have defects in our souls. These all boil down to:

1. a faulty picture of the Creation (including the God at its centre), and of the way He designed it to work, and

2. an imperfect rule book for the business of living.

The picture of life that I (Richard) once carried in my soul centred on the 'fact', based on my experience, that 'love' always had to be earned. More than this, 'love's' demands were onerous. We all need love, and my spirit lived in a soul that said that there was no choice but to work very hard to earn this. My spirit was a prisoner of this belief in my soul. And I wore myself out trying to live by it.

If a more accurate image of God, and of the way He loves us, had been embedded in my soul, my early life would have been very different.

Patterns like this repeat themselves over and over again in different lives. Ill-informed souls force our fallen spirits into living life in a myriad of stressful and fruitless ways.

Four main consequences of soul starvation

Our failure to receive a perfect diet of God's truth-bearing love has these four consequences:

*   it impairs our ability to relate and receive;
*   it stunts our development;
*   it makes us feel cheated;
*   it leads us to look for substitutes.

1. Impaired ability to relate and receive

The most serious casualty of our not receiving into our souls all the truth-bearing love that we were meant to is the quality of our relationships. As a result of our failure to do this, our ability to relate constructively and receptively to God, to other people, and to the Creation becomes increasingly impaired as life goes on.

All human imperfection represents a step down, in one form or other, from the inner perfection found in Jesus the man. Because His soul was God-centred, and truth-filled, He was able to maintain unimpaired relationship with God and with other people, throughout His life.

We can illustrate Jesus' ability to relate in spirit to God and to all aspects of the creation, in a continuously open and whole way, like this (Figure 14):

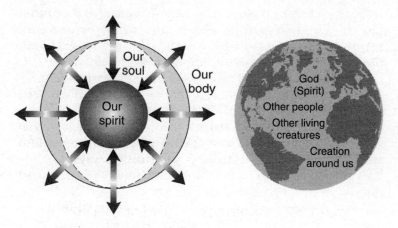

Figure 14

We, however, would look more like Figure 15.

Our failure to receive a full and pure supply of God's truth-bearing love affects our ability to relate and to receive in two ways.

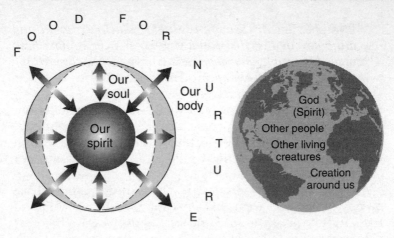

Figure 15

Firstly, it means that we have an inadequate and distorted picture of God in our souls. This is serious because, as we will see in more detail in Part Four, **how we see God dictates how we relate to Him**, and therefore how receptive we are to Him, and to those human agents who come to us in His name. If we like the look of what we see we will embrace them, and receive from them. If not, we will distance ourselves from them, and reject them as a source of at least some of the good things that they might otherwise feed into our souls.

As we have seen, everything our souls receive comes through our spirits' dialogue with their surroundings. Since the Fall, however, we all start life without a relationship of our own with God. Unlike Jesus we are not brought up in God's presence. Until we are 'born again' our spirits have no direct contact with Him. This means that He can have no **direct** input into our souls during our earliest formative years. However, though we may not know God ourselves, we are still surrounded with other people (who have been made in His image), and with His Creation. These all bring something of Him to us. As Romans 1:20 puts it:

> *'Ever since the creation of the world His invisible nature and attributes, that is, His eternal power and divinity, have been made intelligible and clearly discernible in and through the things that have been made – His handiworks.'*

Nothing matches having our own direct, personal relationship with God. But other people, and the Creation around us, reflect Him to us. Because of this we all build some idea of God, and of His perspective on life, into our souls and our inner world-view.

All this is part of God's design. There is no greater calling on any of our lives than that of bearing witness to God and His nature to those around us. Because of the way that God has designed this part of the creative process, we **are all** God's representatives to one another, although this is especially true of parents towards their children. Whether we truly know Him or only know about Him, and whether we are consciously trying to do it or not, or even have any idea that this is happening, we **all** contribute to the way those we have contact with see God.

What this means, however, is that, because of the ravages of sin in this fallen world, the best that any of us can expect to start life with is a second-hand, watered-down perception of who God is and what He is like. He will always seem less wonderful and less attractive to us than He really is. This in turn means that we will not be as close or open to Him, or to His agents of nurture, as He intended.

The second way in which our failure to receive a full and pure supply of truth-bearing love affects our ability to relate, and to receive, is by causing us to build inner defences into our souls.

Our spirits and souls know instinctively what they want. Unless they are continually fed the pure diet that God intended for them there will inevitably be a defensive closing-off.

This second barrier takes the form of mechanisms built into our souls, to shield us from absorbing impurities, and the discomfort that goes with them. Over time, either through repeated experience of the same impurity, or through single strong shocks, a whole series of these mechanisms become fixed in our souls. They are then automatically triggered by people or situations that **look like** those that led to their being set up in the first place.

These defences **are often genuinely effective** in warding off unwelcome intrusion, but they have one major catch. **They always also block out elements of the positive food for nurture that we all need, if we are to mature to a Christ-like wholeness**.

If we were mature and whole, in the way that Christ was, we would be able to make sound, Spirit-guided judgments all the time. These would enable us to receive into ourselves what would be good for us, whilst filtering out what would not. We would be able to wisely use the armour that God provides for us, and which is described by Paul in Ephesians 6. However, our buried and forgotten defences are not similarly sensitive or amenable to our control. Based on past experiences, and driven most commonly by ungodly fear or anger, they cut in haphazardly on their own. As a result, they keep out what would bless us, just as much as they protect us.

It is not only our ability to relate and receive in the first place, but also our ability to sustain relationships with other imperfect people, as Jesus did, that suffers from a lack of God's truth-bearing love. If one element of this soul-food – the truth that God loves each of us unconditionally and continuously, and is always there to meet all of our spiritual, emotional, and physical needs perfectly – had permeated every layer of our souls, as it did Jesus', this would profoundly affect the way that we conducted our daily lives. Like Jesus, we would be constantly open to the healing and re-charging properties of God's love, and so able to remain vulnerable and to carry on embracing others from the heart, despite any insensitivity or rejection that we might experience.

As it is, before we come to Christ, our souls' concept of love is based only on our relationships with people whose love is imperfect. Being 'advised' by those souls that this 'love' is never completely reliable and sufficient, or safe, our spirits take steps to guard themselves from being disappointed or hurt. This makes us inflexibly choosy about who we are open to and how much, including God.

In extreme cases, where our souls receive little or no love or understanding of God, they may 'advise' our spirits to withdraw from all meaningful relationship. This is illustrated in Figure 16.

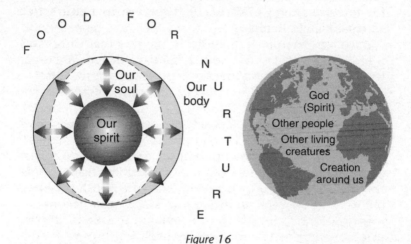

Figure 16

2. Failure to grow up fully

The result of our having a diminished ability to relate and receive is that in some areas of our make-up we actually remain like children.

In his Letter to the Ephesians, Paul tells us that God wants to see us all growing up into the same maturity that Jesus showed. He says that one of the chief consequences of this is that we will *'no longer be children'* (Ephesians 4:14).

The result of the defects in our souls is that every one of us will have missed out. In terms of the food for nurture that we need to grow to an all round maturity, we will have gone hungry. In some cases, we will, quite literally, have starved.

Jane's was a deprived childhood. She received only a fraction of the truth-bearing love that God intends for each of us in childhood. As a result she had grown up to be a highly insecure adult – even to the point of being confused about who she was. This insecurity, together with a proneness to depression, had remained rooted in her make-up right through her time as a wife and mother.

She was aware of these and a whole list of other weaknesses at the time she came to see us. Yet, when we asked her what she would most like Jesus to do for her, she replied quite simply:

> 'I'd like Him to help me to grow up. In many ways I feel just like a child.'

Few people are able to express their need this clearly and succinctly. Yet what Jane said perfectly put its finger on this second effect of being deprived of God's truth-bearing love. Whilst we may reach adulthood looking for all the world grown up on the outside, on the inside we will actually be more like two people – an adult and a child.

Figures 17 and 18 are two more simple diagrams that may help to fix this concept in our minds.

In Figure 17, the black dot in the middle represents each of us at conception. The three broken circles represent proper, well-rounded development in all areas of our make-up at the ages of five, ten, and fifteen; the outer circle represents full maturity. (At around eighteen we should become adults.)

The arrows coming from the centre of the diagram represent growth to maturity in different areas of our make-up. This growth is inextricably linked to the quality of our relationships with God's designated nurturers.

The heavy curves A, B, C represent the actual level of maturity that we have reached in different areas of our make-up.

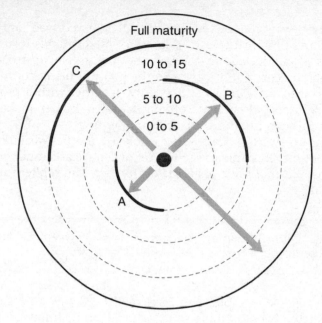

Figure 17

Jesus' wholeness would be represented by a perfectly rounded circle. But our own inner make-up would produce a shape more like that shown in Figure 18.

The shortcomings of human love sources, exacerbated by the inner barriers that we erect, inevitably block off elements of God's food for nurture, and so limit growth in different areas of our make-up.

The result of this is that we are all a mixture of maturity and immaturity, of wholeness and damage, and of health and sickness. We are satisfied adult and deprived child, all at the same time.

Except to the discerning eye, the child mostly only ever appears on the surface when we are under pressure or worn down – at times like these we can no longer conceal this part of ourselves. Nonetheless, the child is there all the time – generating much of our thought-life and behaviour.

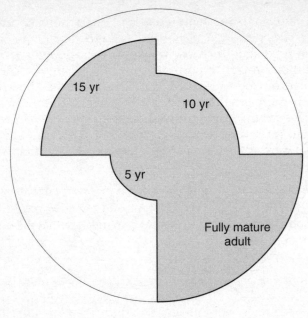

Figure 18

It is God's intention that, in the same way that a lion cub disconnects once and for all from its mother's milk when it becomes sufficiently mature to hunt and to find water for itself, we too should disconnect from our parents as primary sources of nurture when we become young adults. By then, proper nurture will have provided us with a diet that has satisfied our God-given physical, emotional, and spiritual needs as children. We will leave home equipped for the task of living a rich adult life of our own.

We are all immature and hungry in some way. But what perpetuates this state of affairs, even after we have obtained direct access to a God who **is** love, is the defensive barriers that remain in our souls. These are rarely consciously erected against Him. But, **until they are removed they always continue to cut us off from receiving from God.**

Some words that Julia wrote to us clearly and succinctly illustrate this state of affairs.

As a result of being repeatedly, and often violently, raped by her father from little girl to full-grown woman, Julia had put up defence barriers of every kind. Though they had served their protective purpose, they also meant that only a small part of God's intended food for nurture had been able to reach the places that needed it. When we first saw her, she was a young woman of nearly thirty, and had been a Christian for several years. Yet these self-made structures of the soul were still very much in place and doing their work. She wrote:

> 'How the little me and the child me and the adult me longs for God's love. And, at the moment, so much of that me is so empty of that love.'

For most of us, neither our life experience, nor the extent of our inner barriers, nor the level of our starvation, are as extreme as Julia's. Nonetheless, to some degree, we are all like her.

3. Feeling cheated and angry

The Bible tells us that every one of us is made in the image of God. Because of this, we each have an innate sense of what is fair. This means that we know instinctively whether or not we are receiving the quality of nurture that God intends for us.

If we are denied this in any way, we will always register the shortfall. Sometimes we may know exactly how we have been offended against. But, more commonly, we will just be aware of a general feeling of discontent somewhere deep inside us. At times we may try to tell ourselves otherwise, but the feeling will still be there.

The parts of us that have not matured as intended will be characterised by an underlying sense of hunger and dissatisfaction. This will be in marked contrast to the sense of repleteness and contentment that pervades the parts that, having been properly fed, have blossomed into their intended maturity.

For as long as our rightful needs remain unmet, we will continue to feel this hunger for what we have not received. And from our souls will issue a variety of negative emotions, like resentment and self-pity.

The inner mechanism that records our response to the quality of nurture that we receive is like a pair of perfectly sensitive and accurate meters. The first we can call our 'justice meter', and the second our 'anger meter'.

The 'justice meter' reflects how closely our upbringing measures up to God's best for us. The 'anger meter' measures what we feel about this. The lower the reading on the 'justice meter', the higher will be the reading on the 'anger meter'.

Negative readings on these two 'meters' have this important consequence: on the surface we may appear to be on good terms with God and His primary agents of nurture, starting with our parents. But, deeper down, the story will be quite different. Here we will be locked into a kind of long-term cold-war-with-a-purpose against them.

A simple drawing (Figure 19) will help to illustrate what we mean by this.

Figure 19

For as long as we remain deprived of any part of God's intended food for nurture, there will be a child inside us with its hands around the throats of those who it sees as having failed to provide that food. That child will be trying endlessly to accomplish two things. The first is to extract from them what it failed to receive, and still craves. ('You owe me.') The second is to give vent to its anger against those that have failed it. ('I owe you.')

Every shortfall in the truth-bearing love that is our right in some way poisons our relationships with those who should have given it. It also spoils our ability to relate to God, who they represent. Far from loving them from the depths of our being, we are actually waging a cold war with them. The purpose of this war is to finally extract from them what they have owed us all along, and to somehow make them pay for the ways in which they have failed us.

Time and time again, things that those we counsel say to us reveal this condition of the soul.

Like Julia, Sharon also had a deprived childhood. She received little in the way of the praise and encouragement that every child needs. Mostly she was criticised. She asked to see us for help with a deep fear, confusion, and insecurity within herself. Yet, when we asked her face to face what she most wanted Jesus to do for her, she paused, thought deeply, and said:

'I want to be friends with my Mum and Dad.'

In saying what she did Sharon was expressing what, to a greater or lesser extent, is inside each of us, no matter how much we may try to deny it: an unhappy 'inner child' at war with those who have short-changed it.

4. Pursuit of substitutes
Where the needs of our soul are concerned, nothing can take the place of God's truth-bearing love.

However, just as a starving man will eat whatever comes to hand, so we too accept the substitutes that the world and the Devil offer us.

We will be looking at some of these in Part Four. But suffice it to say here that one of the most common is looking to our present-day partners and friends to make up the deficit from the past. This they cannot do.

Pursuing substitutes is a habit that permanently denies our souls what they really need – to be fed from God's hand.

The four effects of soul starvation will all be evident in the personal stories that follow. These give real-life examples of how our experiences in this imperfect world shape our souls, and in doing so affect both our quality of life and our health.

Susan's story

Susan came to see us because she was depressed, depleted, lonely, hurting, and drinking heavily. She had known Jesus for many years, was married to a gentle and dutiful Christian man, and had three beautiful children. She also had everything that she could want materially. But none of this seemed to help.

The Psalmist is right when he says:

> *'O Lord, You have searched me, and You know me.*
> *You know when I sit and when I rise;*
> *You perceive my thoughts from afar.*
> *You discern my going out and my lying down;*
> *You are familiar with all my ways.*
> *Before a word is on my tongue,*
> *   you know it completely, O Lord.*   (Psalm 139:1–4 NIV)

God is love. He is perfectly in tune with us, and with our needs. He wants to have intimate fellowship with us. Nothing can warm our hearts more than knowing this. But, because of her experiences during childhood, there was a little girl inside Susan who had a very different picture of God.

As we have seen, the influence that particular experiences have on our souls, depends on a combination of their individual weight, the number of times that they repeated themselves, and how early they occurred. Sometimes a single event can affect the world-view in our souls out of all proportion to the time it lasts. Most often, however, it is from routine occurrences that repeat themselves over and over again that our souls make up their encyclopaedia for living.

What Susan remembered most about her father was his remoteness. He was also religious, strict, and demanded high standards from his children.

Throughout her childhood she had longed for meaningful communication with him – to really know him and be known by him. This never happened.

When her father did speak to her, Susan would often feel crushed by his sarcastic tongue. 'It seems to me now,' she told us, 'that I was like a puppy dog – always leaping up and trying to lick its master's face. Every now and then, a cuff would come its way, and it would retreat into a corner to lick its wounds, until the next time.'

As a result, part of the picture of life stored in Susan's soul was the 'fact' that men are remote. They give little of themselves, but expect much. Her encyclopaedia for living told her, 'You can't expect any deep and meaningful communication with men. Don't waste time trying, you will just be disappointed. Learn to live without it. Be good. Work hard. Then you will at least earn approval.' To avoid further disappointment and bruising, she withdrew her spirit behind a defensive wall.

This view of men seriously limited Susan's ability to relate to her husband. It dictated the way she saw him, and it dictated the way she saw God. She worked flat out as a wife and mother to earn their approval. But the doors of her heart were firmly closed to the intimacy and love that she really needed from them. Because of the example of her father, she had long since written them off as sources of the kind of close companionship that she craved. By the time she came to see us she was worn out trying to earn approval. At the same time the doors to her soul were firmly closed to the love of God that she had so desperately lacked all her life.

Amanda's story

Another hindrance to relationship that can lodge in our souls is fear of rejection. This, too, prevents our spirits from flowing out fully, even in our closest relationships. It also leads to our erecting defensive barriers behind which we retreat – and starve.

We can be specifically taught to be wary of relationship, but more often this becomes a part of our souls as a result of having being let down by human love sources. Usually there will have been a repeated pattern of betrayal, but in Amanda's case her fear sprang from a single, seemingly trivial event. This took place when she was six.

Amanda adored her grandfather. She believed that he felt the same about her. In many ways he was like a father to her. One day she, her mother, and her younger sister were visiting him at home. Amanda was playing with her sister in the living room, whilst her grandfather sat quietly in a corner, reading a newspaper. Her mother was preparing lunch in the kitchen next door.

Amanda felt hungry and wanted a bar of chocolate to eat. But having had one already, she knew that her mother was unlikely to allow her a second. So she made a secret pact with her sister, who had not eaten anything, that she would go and ask their mother instead – pretending that it was for herself. Their grandfather observed all this going on.

Their mother, guessing what was afoot, returned to the living room and confronted Amanda. She immediately pleaded innocence. But at this point her grandfather intervened. With an expression suddenly devoid of any warmth, and in an angry, condemning voice, he exposed Amanda as a liar. Her mother said nothing.

Her grandfather's severity came as an enormous shock to little Amanda. Until then he had seemed to be as accepting and gentle a person as she could imagine. He had certainly never come down on her in this way before. She read his expression, and what he said, as a complete rejection of her as a person.

During his lifetime, her grandfather never again referred to this incident. He never did anything to show her that she was forgiven, nor did her mother. Her silence at the time of the incident and afterwards seemed to say that, in her eyes, the punishment fitted the crime. Amanda believed that from that moment on her grandfather had stopped loving her, even though in her own eyes her offence had been comparatively trivial.

Because of this, her soul contained the following conclusions about the love of others:

1. It can be withdrawn without warning – no matter how reliable it has seemed in the past.

2. It can be withdrawn arbitrarily for some offences but not others. Gravity is not necessarily a factor.

3. This applies to God's love as much as anyone else's.

Based on these 'facts', Amanda's inner guide to living told her spirit that, no matter what quality of love seems to be on offer, it is always safest to hold back, and guard your heart.

Amanda grew up to be a wholesome and attractive young woman. She drew many people of integrity to herself. She also married a fine, and wholly trustworthy, Christian man. She had every reason to be able to rely on the love of others. She longed for more love, yet something inside her prevented her from wholeheartedly embracing any of them. The grown Christian woman wanted to love and be loved more fully, but was held back by the fearful little girl inside. This applied to her relationship with God as well.

It was only as Amanda listened to our teaching that, for the first time, she began to make the connection between the way she held back in her relationships as an adult and her childhood experience.

Linda's story

Mary Cheney once wrote a little poem:

> Said the robin to the sparrow:
> 'I should really like to know
> Why these anxious human beings
> Rush about and worry so.'

> Said the sparrow to the robin:
> 'Friend, I think it just must be
> That they have no Heavenly Father,
> Such as cares for you and me.'

Amongst the fundamental truths that God wants to reside in the soul of each of us is the fact that He not only exists, but is also in ultimate control of everything around us. What this means is that, in Christ, all will ultimately be well for us. He also wants us to know that He cares about every aspect of our lives, and has the resources to meet every one of our legitimate needs.

Linda was nearly forty, and had been a Christian since her teens. She had three children of her own. But the 'facts' that she still carried in her soul from her childhood gave her neither a sense that God exists, cares, and can meet all our needs, nor the peace and comfort that goes with this. As a result she was subject to high levels of anxiety and depression.

In Linda's case, however, what was lodged in her soul was the result of a state of affairs that had existed throughout her childhood. As a little girl, she had lived with her parents in a house bought for them by her grandfather. He had done this on condition that he was allowed to live there too. Linda described him as: 'a very manipulative and selfish man. He had two breakdowns. He had tantrums. He even threatened suicide. He was always ill, and in the last few years needed a lot of nursing.'

Family life had constantly revolved around this increasingly unpredictable, insensitive, and demanding old man. He suffered, amongst other things, from incontinence. As an impressionable little girl, Linda was regularly confronted with the unpleasant and alarming sight of him rushing semi-naked to the toilet. As she later said: 'I hated him, but was never allowed to say so.'

Linda was not the only one to resent her grandfather's constant controlling presence. It placed great pressure on both her parents as well. They were not given the space that they needed. As a result, the atmosphere in the home was explosive.

Far from feeling wanted and cherished, Linda felt that her presence actually added to the problems her parents had to deal with. The result was a tension-filled home, in which Linda's own needs for love and attention seemed to be a low priority. Her brother described them both as having had 'missed' childhoods.

Amongst the 'facts' that Linda built into her soul were these:

1. Such love as exists is scarce. You cannot expect to be truly liked for yourself, but you can earn toleration.

2. Being your true self can fatally overtax such acceptance as there is.

3. Even the strongest beings struggle to keep control. Therefore there is no real security. Everything is precarious.

4. Assistance and guidance on the journey through life are in short supply. Potential sources of help invariably have to focus their resources on needs greater than yours.

Digesting these 'facts', her soul told her spirit:

1. Do not be your real self, but be whatever makes life easiest for others. This way you will not overtax love sources, and stand the best chance of attracting what little approval there is.

2. Curtail your desire to reach out to others. They simply do not have the resources to respond to you, or to meet

with you, as you would like them to. Essentially you are on your own.

3.   Tread carefully. There are land-mines everywhere.

4.   Life is essentially chaotic, but being perfect keeps things as ordered as they can be.

It is not difficult to see why, from her childhood, Linda came to accept neglect and loneliness as the norm; why she feared that chaos and disruption were always just around the corner; or why she believed that by and large you have to make it on your own in this life. But it was these messages, operating relentlessly on her spirit from the deepest layers of her soul, that were the cause of the anxiety and depression that dogged her as an adult.

Catherine's story

In general, the earlier and the more often we experience things, the greater will be their influence on the landscape of our souls.

However, as we have seen from Amanda's story, single experiences, too, can have a significant effect on the quality of our relationships. Catherine's story shows how such experiences, even when they come late in our formative years, can reinforce and compound 'facts' already implanted in our souls.

Catherine was a married woman of about forty when she came to see us. She had always been aware of having problems in relating to men. She was happily married to a strongly committed Christian man, who was by all accounts gentle and caring. Despite this, she still found emotional and physical openness and intimacy difficult.

As she listened to our teaching on the effect of past experiences on present behaviour, the Holy Spirit began to show Catherine what had caused her inhibitions.

On completion of her school and college education, she had decided that she would like to spend her first few working years abroad, before settling down at home.

The Far East attracted her, because of the novelty of its culture and customs. She went to live in Hong Kong, where she found herself a job and an apartment of her own to live in.

As a young woman who had lived all of her life in familiar surroundings, with family and friends close at hand, she had led a comparatively sheltered life. Her new situation thus represented a voyage into the substantially unknown. Attractive and gregarious, she was keen to meet new people and to make friends. And it was not long before this happened. However, one evening she made the mistake of inviting a young man, whom she had seen only once or twice, but who seemed a trustworthy person, back to her apartment. They became affectionate, and, despite the fact that she resisted throughout, he had forced sexual intercourse upon her.

The shock and trauma of this experience had been immense for Catherine. There were no close friends at hand to talk to about it. Instead she quickly buried the memory of it inside herself.

She had never once consciously recalled the incident during the intervening years. Nevertheless, it had made its mark on her soul.

It seems that as a child Catherine had not felt particularly well understood by her father, and that he had unwittingly hurt her feelings on numerous occasions. What she experienced that night in Hong Kong took the 'facts' about men that were already stored in her soul a stage further. To the little girl and the young woman in her, these 'facts' meant that, whatever first impressions might indicate, there was an unbridgeable gulf between the male of the species and the female. It was an extremely high-risk group to do any kind of business of the heart with. In particular, because of that one most traumatic experience, sexual intimacy with a man became inextricably associated with physical and emotional pain.

Again, it is not difficult to see how and why the encyclopaedia in Catherine's soul impaired her ability, as a woman and a wife, to relate to men. It held a poor image of men, and a defensive strategy developed to keep them well away from vulnerable territory. Even when this strategy was no longer needed, it was still ruling her spirit, and starving her soul.

Summarising earthly soul-building

We are all flawed to the very roots of our being.

The delicate mechanism that goes to make up a human being was designed, right from conception, to develop within an environment of perfect unconditional love and complete sinlessness. This has not been reality for any of us. The person that each of us is today is a natural consequence of our being brought up in what is, by God's standards, an imperfect environment for nurture. At the same time, because of our fallen nature, we have all reacted imperfectly to the imperfect world around us, making choices that Christ would not have made, and thus building un-Christ-likeness deep into our own make-up.

Whether we have been aware of it or not, the exercise of choice, flowing from the free will that God has given each of us, has played an enormous part in making us the fundamentally imperfect people that we are.

It is the selection of 'facts', and the conclusions that **we draw from them, and allow to lodge in our souls**, that in the end decide how our souls direct our spirits, and the way we live our lives. The deeper the level at which 'facts' and conclusions are stored the greater their influence.

Figure 20 illustrates this. The black dots represent spirit-imprisoning contents that may have become lodged within its structure at different times. The soul then 'speaks' these contents to the spirit, causing it to live a life that is less than God's best.

Our souls can free or imprison us. They can enable us to be fully the people we were created to be, or they can restrict and control us.

When I (Richard) was a little boy, I lived with my family in Kuala Lumpur, the capital of West Malaysia. Frequent visits to England, first for holidays and then to attend boarding

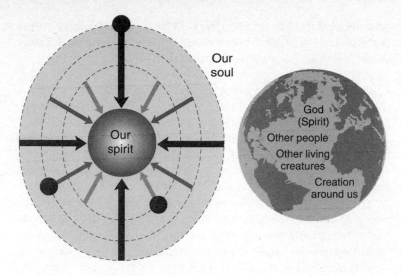

Figure 20

school, meant I was something of an international commuter. The eight thousand mile journey by air was always a momentous event. However, what is now little more than an overnight flight then took up to two whole days! For an active little boy, confined to his seat for all that time, potentially the greatest problem was boredom. Because of this, I always went armed with a selection of books and games to occupy me.

Amongst these were a series of small moving puzzles, sealed in little wooden boxes with glass fronts. One of my favourites consisted of a walled maze and a small silver ball. The object was to roll the ball as quickly as possible from one end of the maze to the other, without losing it down any of a succession of awkwardly placed holes along the way.

This puzzle provides a useful illustration of the way in which our souls can affect the life of our spirits. Our souls can become a maze that checks, frustrates, and discourages our spirits.

Our spirits should be comfortable within us. They should be free to be themselves. However, the messages our souls give our spirits can cause them all sorts of discomfort, and restrict their natural movement. They can bombard them with fear and confusion, sometimes even causing them to 'break down' or to think suicidal thoughts.

The strongest and most fulfilled spirit is one that is free – free to be itself. It is also the foundation of a healthy body.

The contents of the soul can so surround and control the spirit as to rob it of much or all of its freedom. They can imprison the spirit, and significantly limit its ability to actively express itself. This, in turn, can lead to physical ill-health.

For example, a healthy spirit is one that, amongst other things, freely expresses emotion. An imprisoned spirit will often bottle this up. It is widely accepted within the medical profession that some forms of arthritis have this storing of emotions at their roots.

Naturally we prefer to experience pleasant emotions, but others are just as much a part of everyday life. So it is with anger – our natural, God-given emotional response to injustice. A free spirit will express anger as it arises. This is as it should be. An imprisoned spirit, on the other hand, will often keep it contained within us.

The soul may give any one of a selection of reasons to the spirit to prevent it expressing its anger. It may tell the spirit that this will bring rejection. It may tell the spirit that to express anger is not to love. Whatever the reason put forward, this storing of energy eventually overloads our bodies. This, in turn, can manifest itself in pain and swelling in the bones and joints, or in other forms of physical ill-health.

Truth versus lies

When discussing the kind of spirit-imprisoning information that we can accumulate in our souls, we have often used the word 'fact' – but in inverted commas.

A fact is something that is generally accepted as representing reality. In this sense every genuine fact is a truth. But the one thing that every 'fact' in our souls that imprisons our spirits has in common is that it is actually **not** the whole truth.

My (Richard's) soul used to contain the spirit-imprisoning 'fact' that love is a commodity that always has to be earned. It may have been true that every so-called love source that I had encountered in my formative years had exacted a price in return for his or her love. But to surmise from this that a person who loved me all the time, no matter what I did, simply did not exist was to carry a lie within my soul.

Whilst the love of every person that we have ever met may have its price, God's love (and indeed that of some of our fellow human beings!) is actually free. He always loves and likes us – no matter what we do or fail to do. This is the whole truth. It is the full picture. Had I carried this in my soul, my spirit (the real me) would have been free – free from having to earn love, and free from the depressing thought that, for as long as I was failing to please love sources, I was not loved.

Truth in the soul always leads to freedom for the spirit. The whole truth frees it completely. This is why Jesus says to Christians:

> *'You will know the truth, and the truth will make you free.'*
> (John 8:32 NRSV)

God has always wanted our spirits free. He has always wanted us free to be ourselves – the people He created us to be. This is why the Psalmist says of Him:

> *'Surely You desire truth in the inner parts.'*
> (Psalm 51:6 NIV)

We need a miracle!

If we look at ourselves in the light of the process of development described in this chapter, it shows us two things. The first is that the person that each of us is today is the product of a construction process. The second is that this process consists, essentially, of our interacting with our surroundings generally, and with certain key people in particular.

We can see, furthermore, that the inevitable result of our own innate waywardness as builders, and the imperfection of those who influence us, is to produce edifices that contain a series of built-in flaws. These flaws adversely affect the quality of our relationships. This in turn adversely affects our spiritual, emotional, and physical health – a state of affairs that will continue for as long as the flaws are in place.

We have all failed, in some way or another, to absorb the full measure of the food for nurture that God prescribes for perfect human development. Whether this was due to short-comings on the part of God's chosen agents of nurture to us or to barriers for which we are responsible, the end result is the same for all of us. We have failed to mature into a full, Christ-like wholeness. Instead we are inwardly stunted and malformed. From our roots upward, we are founded and structured not on God's best, but on an impure and incomplete intake, that undermines our potential to be completely whole and healthy.

The result of all this is that we need a fundamental rebuild to bring us the Christ-like wholeness that God desires for us. Only this, and not superficial patching, will enable us to become fully the people He created us to be.

The natural process of development has had its chance. Time has moved on. We cannot re-create our family home or become again the children we once were. Even if we could, the people around us would still be much the same, and would be likely to fail us again in similar ways. In the natural order of things, no rerun is available. Our only hope for wholeness to the deepest level is that some form of super-natural reconstruction is available – some means by which the faulty brickwork of the past can be dismantled, and reconstituted as it should have been in the first place.

The good news is that every one of us **can** have just such a radical rebuild, through the Cross of Christ and the power of the Holy Spirit of God.

The next chapter explains how.

PART TWO

THE SOLUTION

Chapter 4

Supernatural Reconstruction

'He restores my soul.'
(Psalm 23:3 NIV)

*'His intention was **the perfecting ... of the saints** ... that [we might arrive] at **really mature manhood** – the completeness of personality which is nothing less than the standard height of **Christ's own perfection** – the measure of the stature of the fullness of the Christ and **the completeness found in Him.'***
(Ephesians 4:12–13)

*'For this reason, I bow my knees before the Father ... May He grant you out of the rich treasury of His glory to be strengthened and reinforced with mighty power in the inner man **by the (Holy) Spirit [Himself]** – **indwelling your innermost being and personality**. May Christ, through your faith [actually] ... make His permanent home – in your hearts! May you be **rooted deep in love and founded securely on love**, that you may have the power ... to ... grasp with all the saints ... what is the breadth and length and height and depth [of the love of Christ]; [that you may really come] to know – practically, **through experience for yourselves** – [this love], which far surpasses mere knowledge (without experience); that you may be filled (**through all your being**) unto all the fullness of God – [that is] may have the richest measure of the divine Presence, and become **a body wholly filled and flooded with God Himself!'***
(Ephesians 3:14–19)

God's goal for us

The first of the two extracts from Paul's Letter to the Ephesians, quoted above, reminds us how far-reaching God's plan to transform us really is. He wants us as mature and whole as Jesus was!

God's part in the process

We have already said that, rather than trying ever harder to study and to imitate Jesus, becoming whole means **allowing God to change us**.

But what exactly does this entail? How precisely does He mean to go about this?

The answer is folded into the second of the two extracts from Ephesians. It lies in the way Paul prays.

His prayer, divinely inspired like the rest of Scripture, is in fact a prayer for inner transformation. Paul is praying for the whole family of Christ at Ephesus, but his prayer can apply to us all.

We are all *'rooted and grounded'* (NRSV) in something less than pure, truth-bearing love. Understanding this, Paul prays that we would, from our very foundations upwards, *'be rooted deep in love and founded securely on love'*. He asks the One who invented the very concept of fatherhood to send the Holy Spirit to infuse and occupy our *'innermost being and personality'* with God's pure love. Through this we will be able (or as Paul puts it, *'have power'*) to *'grasp with all the saints what is the breadth and length and height and depth'* of that love – to *'really come to know* [it] *practically,* **through experience for** [ourselves]*'*.

Put another way, Paul asks God, who is beyond time, to revise our past experiences supernaturally, and make us the same as if we had experienced perfect nurture from the beginning!

This is what being changed really means. This is what God is offering us. No more and no less. He is offering to answer Paul's prayer, and to send His Holy Spirit to inject His perfect, truth-bearing love supernaturally into the places inside us that missed out on it during the natural process of development.

Once this love has done its work, our whole being will become securely founded, from its roots upward, on the perfect nourishment that God always intended for us in the first place. Our very souls, which have been *'rooted in'* and *'founded on'* the imperfect nourishment that the world has fed us, will be restored!

If we think for a moment about this approach of God's to changing us, we will see that, in essence, it constitutes a re-run of the natural process of human development – a kind of turning back of the clock, in order to put things right.

We can illustrate this by looking at Figure 21 – a diagram from the previous chapter:

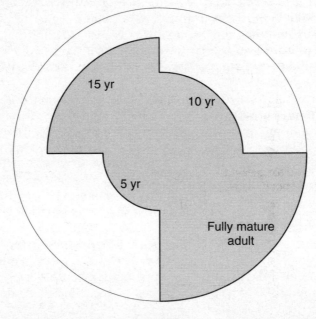

Figure 21

In this diagram, the feint outer circle represents a perfect state of wholeness and maturity – the kind found in Christ.

The grey shape, on the other hand, represents us as we actually are. In some respects we have come to a healthy maturity, in others our growth has been stunted, and we have remained childish.

God's approach to healing this damage is, by the power of His Spirit, to bring perfect nourishment to the parts of us that did not receive it during the natural process of development.

What God's approach to healing really amounts to, in practical terms, is His taking us back in time and feeding the stranded child that still lives in us, and so enabling us to develop as we should have done in the first place. The difference is that this time we have a source of perfect nurture available to us. It is as if God shoulders the unfulfilled responsibilities of all those human agents that we were given to nourish us in the past, and carries them out Himself, retrospectively, giving us a second chance to grow up to healthy maturity.

This process, which we have been privileged to see at work over and over again, can be illustrated as follows (Figure 22):

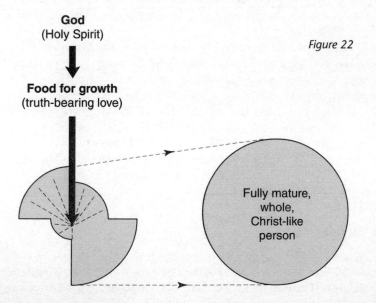

God
(Holy Spirit)

Figure 22

Food for growth
(truth-bearing love)

Fully mature, whole, Christ-like person

It is a wonderful thing to witness the Holy Spirit ministering directly to the damaged child inside people, giving them what they missed out on the first time around, and enabling them to become fully what they were always meant to be. The landscape of people's souls is transformed – sometimes in minutes.

The majority of those whose stories we tell in this book were touched in this dramatic way. We will be focusing on their particular experiences – including, in this chapter, those of three people that we have already met – because they illustrate so strikingly how the Holy Spirit can minister 'beyond time' to the child inside us, and change our souls. But before we do, we want to enter a caution.

We want to say clearly that the Holy Spirit is infinitely versatile. He has many ways of bringing the healing touches that we need – each one tailor-made for the individual concerned. Sometimes He comes in so gradually and gently, over a period, that we are not aware at the time that this is happening. Only later do we realise that we are different, perhaps because of the comments of a friend. At other times, He works so instantly and powerfully that the change is unmistakable.

We emphasise this here because, when our own time comes to receive the Holy Spirit's transforming work, it is important that we are openly expectant. It is only human to want instant results, but this can be seriously counter-productive. **If we have decided in advance how and when we want the Holy Spirit to work, we may limit His freedom to move as He thinks best, or keep Him out altogether**.

Bearing in mind this need to let God be God, we now turn to look at four striking examples of His Holy Spirit at work.

Linda

Linda was the young mother who came to see us because she could no longer cope with the level of depression and anxiety that was affecting her. At the root of this was a soul formed in a home filled with tension and trauma, centring on a demanding grandfather. No one really had the time or resources to properly meet her needs as a little girl. She had felt very alone, and was not even sure that she was really liked at all. She described her childhood as dark. It was as if, she said, 'happiness had been buried in a grave'.

Here is how Linda described the Holy Spirit coming to the damaged little girl, who still lived inside her, feeding her with what she had missed, and so changing the contents of her soul:

'I'm not sure if vision is the right word, but that's how I think of it, and it was very real. After you prayed for me, I remember sitting back on the comfy sofa and feeling as though I was sort of floating. I was about five or six again, and I was skipping down the long hallway of my childhood home. I know I was little because of the size of the hall.

It started off dark, as I had remembered it, but as I approached the kitchen door it became much brighter and sunnier. I was smiling and skipping and the door opened and Jesus was in the kitchen. I knew it was Him, and He took my hands and started to skip and dance around with me in the kitchen.

I felt incredibly happy. He joined me on my level and wanted to have fun with me.

I led Him into the garden and we skipped up to the cherry blossom tree. As a child I often played under the tree when it was in blossom. I'd always wanted someone to shake the branches, because the blossom came down in showers. Jesus shook the branches and the petals showered down. I was laughing and jumping in them.

We went further up the garden and He pushed me on the swing. It was just great fun. I knew I had His undivided attention. He picked me up off the swing. He held me, gave me a big cuddle, and said, "I'm going now, but I'll come back ... and I'll never be far away." I waved and it felt fine that He'd gone.

I have no idea how long the "vision" lasted in real time. I often "play it back" in my mind and experience again the happiness and peace and sheer joy that goes with it. It made me feel totally loved and accepted, and it was amazing to feel God's love so first hand.'

At a stroke, by the power of His Holy Spirit, God supernaturally revised the experience of the little girl inside Linda. He caused her to become *'rooted deep in love and founded securely on'* perfect love, where previously she had been 'rooted in' and 'founded on' something quite different. He perfectly discerned and personally met her needs, retrospectively injecting into her what should have been routine ingredients in her original development. The Holy Spirit ministered previously unknown truth to Linda – truth about God and truth about herself. As a result she came to know deep inside what He was really like, and what He really thought of her. She came to know that He really was there for her, had time for her, and loved her for who she was.

Anne

God can always be relied on absolutely to play His part in bringing us whatever healing we need. However, for reasons that we may not always be able to understand fully, even when supernatural touches of the kind we are describing do come, they may not always come when we think they should. They may still be a part of His healing plan for us, but nonetheless be delayed.

The experience of Anne, another young mother, who came to us with problems of anxiety and low self-esteem, provides a good example of this.

We had spent several sessions explaining to Anne the kind of love that God had for her. We had also told her about some of the occasions when we had seen the Holy Spirit transforming people by bringing this love to the needy 'inner child' in them. We explained how He often did this by simply bringing the presence of Jesus to spend time with the child and to play with it.

In the counselling room with us, in obedience and expectation, Anne did everything that she needed to do in order to make it possible for God to work in her in this way. (We will be describing in detail, in the next chapter and those after it, just what this entails.) But it was not until a full year later that she wrote to say this:

'Shortly after leaving you, I went on a worship conference in Brighton. I love conferences – especially worship – but I had no idea how God was going to bless me! There were some talks, and I learned so much again about the Father's love. Then a musician introduced a new song. I couldn't believe it, it was called "Dancing with the Father"!

As he was playing and singing, I couldn't stop smiling. Then I began to laugh. The words were:

I'm dancing with my Father
He's throwing me up in the air
I'm dancing – me and my Father
I like it up there with my Father
I like it up there with my Father.

Well, it was just as if I was being thrown up in the air, and I was giggling. It was such FUN! For months after that I giggled every time I heard this song!!

Since then God the Father has let me play – not in my outward life (that's been busy and demanding and tough), but when I am spending time with Him quietly in prayer. Recently He showed me myself and Him playing some kind of board game. It looked like marbles. I was looking up to Him and then I would giggle and roll the marble. (I was about four or five.) I would then look a bit anxious and would look up again to my Father, but He wasn't anxious. He was smiling at me. He then rolled the marble back to me and we laughed together.

I believe I am that age at the moment, in His eyes. He hasn't let me go from there. I'm glad, for the time being. I want Him to keep showing me things.

I felt that He was letting me know how to play this game; that I had to keep looking up to ask Him the next step; that He wasn't going to be frowning or refusing to play or to pass the marble; and that it was okay if I made a mistake.

This is all I need to know. This gets me through everything else. When I get 'ground down' I go to Him and let Him know, and try not to feel guilty. This bit is still not easy, but the "game scene" helps me so much to do it.'

The setting in which God did His healing work was different – daily life rather than the counselling room. But once again we saw Him coming, by the power of His Holy Spirit, to the fear-filled little girl of the past. As He did, He began to re-anchor Anne in His perfect love.

Amanda

Truth is the key ingredient of God's soul-nourishing love. This is primarily truth about Him, and truth about ourselves.

However, Amanda's experience shows us the Holy Spirit bringing healing truth of another kind home to a person's soul: truth about a past event.

Amanda was the young mother who came for help, after hearing our teaching, because of a deep difficulty in trusting the love of people close to her. She was aware that this held her back from fully loving both those people and God.

The Holy Spirit had shown her that the root of this was fear caused by a childhood incident, in which her especially adored grandfather, who had long since died, appeared to abruptly stop loving her.

We will leave it to Amanda to describe, as she did to all of those present at the seminar, how the Holy Spirit brought healing truth to her soul:

'The Holy Spirit took me back to that room. My grandfather was standing there, just as he had been on that awful day. It was so simple ... Jesus was just standing there next to me. Then He walked over to where my grandfather was. It was as if He wanted to show me something about my grandfather. As my eyes followed Him, He reached out one hand to him and one hand to me, as if drawing us together. I was able to look at my grandfather's face for the first time since that day. As I did, I saw that it was the same old face that I had always known before – smiling and warm. I was able to run to him with open arms...'

(Amanda was unable to continue her account beyond this point, so overcome was she with tears of joy. When we asked her to describe how she had felt since the 'reconciliation', she could only let out a 'Wooooo...' sound – as if to indicate that she had been walking on air! The whole room broke into spontaneous applause and cheers.)

Embedded in Amanda's soul had been the belief that, because of what she had done, her grandfather had ceased to love her from that moment on. As a result, all loving had become a dangerous thing to do. However, in His own unique way, the Holy Spirit brought the truth home to her, and, in Amanda's own words, 'got it all sorted'.

Catherine

Where we need it, God longs to heal our souls. There is no doubt about **His** willingness and ability to play His part in this process of change. What is far less certain is whether we will play **our** part.

It took Catherine, whose story also we told in Chapter 3, twenty years to take the steps that allowed God to heal her soul of the effects of her father's insensitivity, and then being raped. When she did, the effect was immediate and dramatic.

As we prayed for Catherine, she began to re-experience all the thoughts and feelings of that terrible evening twenty years before. God knew that these had been bottled up ever since then, and needed to be released. It was as if she **were** that twenty-one-year-old once more. Pain and fear showed on her face, as she tried in vain to resist her attacker. From time to time she would describe events, as she relived the feelings of disgust and loss and dirtiness that every woman in her position feels. All the while, tears ran quietly down her cheeks.

The minutes passed. Then, slowly but surely, these emotions began to subside. There were still tears flowing quietly down her cheeks, but the expression on her face was somehow different. Relief and peace and a deep joy were taking the place of anguish and discomfort, until eventually she seemed to have come to a place of the sweetest inner peace.

She opened her eyes, and we waited eagerly to know what had happened. This is what she told us:

> 'I was all alone in the bathroom. I was holding a sponge. I was trying to wash myself clean. Then Jesus was there. He took the sponge from my hand, and, ever so tenderly, began to wash me. Jesus was washing me clean!'

She did not need to say more. The atmosphere in the room was already so charged with a sense of the deep healing that she was receiving. It was as if we too were being embraced in the same tender arms as Catherine.

Time and space do not permit us to describe all the instances of the Spirit of God working in this way that we have been privileged to see. However, we hope that these few examples provide a feel for what He can do to change the very deepest levels of our souls – enabling us to relate to Him and others in a new way, and to receive what our souls need for us to become the people we were always meant to be.

This is an exciting prospect for all of us. But there is more. The fact that God can work in this way makes it possible for us to become one day, as the Amplified Bible puts it, *'wholly filled and flooded with God Himself'* – in other words, just like Jesus!

Full Christ-likeness – an attainable goal

Wonderful though stories like Linda, Anne, Amanda, and Catherine's are, they represent only single stages in their walks to complete wholeness. Having read them, we may still question whether we can ever come close to knowing just what it must have been like to have been Jesus the man. All the power of our imagination may not enable us to visualise ever living in a house like the one that His soul provided for His spirit. To the extent that this is so, it is because the formative periods of our lives are so different from His. But this can all change.

Especially for those of us starting out on this journey, an incident from the life of the great nineteenth century man of faith – evangelist, preacher, and founder of orphanages in the West Country – George Muller, provides just one illustration of how advanced this process can become in human beings.

In his biography of Muller, *Delighted In God*, Roger Steer describes how, in August 1877, Muller and his wife set sail aboard a ship called the *Sardinian* for a speaking tour in the United States:

> Off Newfoundland the weather turned cold and the ship's progress was seriously retarded by fog. The captain had been on the bridge for twenty-four hours when something happened which was to revolutionise his life. George Muller appeared on the bridge.
>
> 'Captain, I have come to tell you I must be in Quebec by Saturday afternoon.'
>
> 'It is impossible,' said the captain.
>
> 'Very well,' said Muller, 'if your ship cannot take me, God will find some other way – I have never broken an engagement for fifty-two years. Let us go down into the chart-room and pray.'
>
> The captain wondered what lunatic asylum Muller had come from.

'Mr Muller,' he said, 'do you know how dense this fog is?'

'No, my eye is not on the density of the fog, but on the living God, who controls every circumstance of my life.'

Muller then knelt down and prayed simply. When he had finished the captain was about to pray, but Muller put his hand on his shoulder, and told him not to:

'First, you do not believe He will; and second, I believe He has, and there is no need whatever for you to pray about it.'

The captain looked at Muller in amazement.

'Captain,' he continued, 'I have known my Lord for fifty-two years, and there has never been a single day that I have failed to get an audience with the King. Get up, captain, and open the door, and you will find the fog is gone.'

The captain walked across to the door and opened it. The fog had lifted . . . On the Saturday, as they drew near Quebec, the *Sardinian* fired her guns as a signal of her approach.

None of us carries the complete soul-knowledge of God that Jesus did. None of us is as certain as He was of His Father's existence, His control over everything, and His perspective on how life on Earth should be lived. But when we consider, as we have been in this chapter, God's desire, set out in the Bible, to make all believers like Jesus; when we see the evidence of just what He can do, by the power of the Holy Spirit, to change the souls of ordinary people like ourselves; and when, finally, we look at the example of mature men of God like George Muller, we can see that Christ-like wholeness, confidence, and oneness with God are not the impossible dream that we may have thought they were.

Trusting God's Word, and daring to believe that what He has done in others He can do in us as well, we now turn to look at **what we must do** to make this possible.

Chapter 5

The Part We Must Play

Christian healing, according to the Bible, is essentially this: the progressive removal from our system of all that is not perfectly Christ-like, and its replacement with what is. In other words, it is an exchange. Through this exchange we give away those things inside ourselves that do not help us to lead the 'full life' that God wants for each of us, and receive instead the things that do. As the Bible says:

> 'He will give you, through His great power, everything you need for living a truly good life ... His own glory and ... goodness ... and ... His own character.' (2 Peter 1:3–4 LB)

The process of healing is very like the original process of being 'born again'.

When we are 'born again' the Holy Spirit comes to live in us. He establishes an unshakeable foothold within us, but also trails a line back to God behind Him. This line provides a direct, two-way channel of communication between us and God. It is much like a telephone cable. But it also has the qualities of a drip-feed – through it the Holy Spirit can daily feed God's truth-bearing love into us. This means that, from that moment on, we can begin to receive a fresh supply of His wholeness and health. This includes His way of thinking, feeling, and behaving, as well as truth as He sees it.

Another way of describing being 'born again' is as a loving invasion of an individual's inner being, together with a permanent linking of that person to God. To use the language of space travel, God both docks with the 'spaceship' that is a particular person, and comes aboard. However, in order for this linking invasion to take place, we have to make some room for Him within ourselves. To do this we have to clear out things that are not 'of Him', in that they are against His nature and ways – what the Bible calls sin.

God provides us with specific tools for this purpose, and they give us all that we need to accomplish it.

How life-changing our conversion is depends on the extent to which we clear out our sin and create space for God to come and fill us with Himself.

If, after our initial conversion, we want more of God inside us, the principle is the same. We may call it 'being healed', rather than 'being born again' or 'being saved', but it is simply the same process taking place more deeply and widely within us. **It is converting deeper and deeper levels of our character and make-up, in order to bring the whole of us into line with a conscious decision, made when we first invited Jesus in, that He should reign in our lives**.

Other than this, the mechanics of the process of healing or reconstruction by the power of the Holy Spirit are the same as for initial conversion. It is simply that, becoming aware of additional ways in which we are not like Jesus, and wanting more of His wholeness, we need to create further space within ourselves.

Just as we did at conversion, we must use the tools provided by God to further empty ourselves, and to create the additional space that God needs if He is to inject more of His truth-bearing love into us. If we do not, we will actually rule ourselves out of experiencing further permanent inner change.

It is true that we are the victims of a sinful world. But, as we described in Chapter 3, we have all reacted imperfectly to the imperfect world around us. We have made decisions and drawn conclusions that Christ would not have, and woven them into our souls. So, our sinful and damaged inner make-up is the product of our own choices, as is the commensurate loss of the full life that God intends for each of us. What is inside us is our property. We alone can give it up to God to change. He can repeatedly urge us to do so, and tell us of the rewards. But only **we** can actually do it.

Jesus was God's prime ambassador of the full life. He demonstrated it in action. He offered it freely to us. But from the very start of His earthly ministry, He said:

> *'Repent – that is, change your mind for the better, heartily amend your ways, with abhorrence of your past sins – for the kingdom of heaven is at hand.'* (Matthew 4:17)

In these words Jesus offers us all we could ever want in terms of inner renewal. But to get it we must first do something ourselves. We must **reverse** wrong choices of the past.

Convenient though it might be to think it so, free will and choice are not exceptionally suspended during the healing process. The same freedom of choice that has played such an important part in making us what we are must be exercised in deciding what we are to become. We are called to review past decisions, and often in some detail.

For healing and change of the deepest, most enduring kind to take place, some things need to be done that only we can do. **If we do not do them, such change can never happen**. God longs to make us like Jesus. He designed human life. He gave us the natural process of development through which each of us can grow to full Christ-like wholeness and maturity. Where things go wrong in this process, and we sustain damage to our souls as a result, He is then more than willing, and completely able, to put this right supernaturally, and to restore us to being the people that He always intended us to be. If this does not happen, it is never for lack of willingness or ability on His part. It is simply because, **by our own choice**, there remain within us insurmountable obstacles and barriers to His working.

What we have to say now is perhaps the most important thing in the whole of this book.

> **In our experience, the single biggest obstacle to radical change taking place within the Body of Christ today is its failure to recognIse that we each have an active part to play in the process of our own reconstruction.**

The Bible teaches us time and time again just how vital our participating in this way is to our own transformation. A reluctance to take this teaching seriously and act on it is the main obstacle to our receiving all the inner change that is rightfully ours in Christ. Over and over again a mixture of ignorance, pride, fear, and just plain laziness prevents God from bringing us what we want.

Preparing ourselves for transformation

When we say that we want healing, whether it be of the spirit, the mind, the emotions, or the body, what we are really asking is to become more like Christ as He was when He was on this Earth as a human being. We are looking for more of His perfect wholeness to become a part of our own make-up, including His ability to commune with God and with men. We want to be rid of un-Christ-likeness inside ourselves, and to have Christ's perfection take its place.

These are precisely the terms in which the Bible offers healing. It does this in many places, but nowhere more clearly or emphatically than in 1 John 1:9. This says:

> *'If we confess our sins, he is faithful and just and will forgive us our sins and purify us from **all unrighteousness**.'*
> (NIV)

Christ, the man, was perfectly righteous. Thus, in offering us purification from all unrighteousness, the Bible is saying that we can actually have every last little thing within us, that is not perfectly Christ-like, removed. If you combine this with Paul's prayer in Ephesians that we might be filled, quite simply, full of God, you have the principle of exchange that is at the heart of Christian healing.

The words of 1 John 1:9 are familiar ones. This may be because they are habitually used in church services, in the Anglican liturgy especially, as a lead-in to the General Confession. However, despite this, the depth of healing and change that they offer is rarely brought out. Instead they are treated as if they were meant to apply only to the conscious sins of our recent past – the things which, if we think back for a few moments (all the time that most services allow), we remember having done wrong in the previous few days.

Of course they **can** apply to these sins, but they also apply to the wrong choices, decisions, and conclusions of years ago that have made us what we are today. So we should also see them as saying something like this:

> 'If we confess every way that, throughout the course of our lives, we have not reacted to people or to situations in a perfectly Christ-like way, and so have built our souls imperfectly, He is faithful and just and will forgive us our sins and purify us from all the unrighteousness, or un-Christ-likeness, that we have accumulated since the day of our conception – together with all the sickness of body, soul, and spirit that this has caused us.'

Amplifying John's words in this way, brings out the full extent of what they offer. It shows their sufficiency as a solution to the following three facts of life, which the Bible underlines:

1. By our nature, from conception, we have a propensity to react to the imperfect world around us, in an un-Christ-like, or sinful, manner (Psalm 58:3). As a result we can accumulate un-Christ-likeness and damage of all kinds within ourselves.

2. Sin (through the Fall) is at the root of all 'sickness' of spirit, soul, and body.

3. God's law says that a man will reap what he sows.

A God of mercy, not memory lapses

Forgetting either past sin against us, or our own sinful reaction to it, is not a solution. At any given moment we may be unaware of particular sins of the past, but that does not mean that they are in any way dealt with. To be released from the sins of the past always involves a conscious recognition and an owning of that sin before God. Lack of awareness of past sin or, as 1 John 1:8 puts it, claiming to be without sin, achieves nothing more than self-delusion.

There are three reasons why we may be unaware of past sin. These are:

1.   Lapse of time and a faulty memory.

2.   Denial – a mechanism we often employ to try to escape the guilt or discomfort of past sin.

3.   Our fallen nature – which means that sinning can come so naturally that, even at the time we are committing it, we do not notice that this is happening.

Whatever the reason for our having lost sight of past sin, it continues to affect us, keeping un-Christ-like structures in place within us, until it is dealt with in God's way. All sin involves choices. So God, respecting our free will, must wait for us to reverse those choices. Only then can He take that sin away, and dismantle its consequences in our make-up. As we shall see in a later chapter, God is more than capable of enabling us to recognise, own, and surrender past sin that still needs to be given up to Him.

Salvador Dali once painted a picture of a watch as if it were floating in space and disintegrating. All the parts that made up its mechanism had become separated from each other, but were still sufficiently clustered for it to be identifiable as one watch. Depicted in this way, much more of the watch was visible than we would normally see.

When we look at ourselves, we see ourselves much as we would see a fully assembled watch. Only the exterior surfaces are visible. We see none of the layers of cogs and springs that constantly affect what happens on the clock face.

For us, the things of yesterday, including our past sins, have a tendency to grow pale and to disappear. It is as if, in spiritual terms, we look at ourselves in the mirror today and see only what is at the surface. There are certainly situations in which we become momentarily what we once were, and may still be under the surface – for example in a dream that recalls childhood feelings that we realise are still with us. However, it is the person that we are here and now, both physically and in terms of what we think and do, that dominates our attention.

We often fail to use the tools that God has given us to clear out past sin because we think that we have irretrievably forgotten the past, or at any rate sufficient of it to make this an impossible task. Conveniently, therefore, we assume that what we seem to have forgotten God will have forgotten too. But this is not so. He does not forget, nor does He allow us to do so as an alternative to surrendering past sin. Rather than forgetting, He sees us – even the deep parts of our make-up – as we see that Dali watch, spread out and three-dimensional. Everything, including the inner wear and tear, are visible to Him. He is beyond time and never forgets. To Him there is not one iota of difference between unconfessed sin of today and unconfessed sin of ten, twenty, or even fifty years ago. Both are live issues in His book – affecting our inner make-up and our relationship with Him, until dealt with through the forgiveness made available by the Cross. Time does not cause any of our past to fade or blur in His memory, even though we may not readily be able to put a finger on all of it ourselves.

The good news is that this means that He is able to remind us, by the working of His Holy Spirit, of all that we need to know in order to clear a space for Him at the deeper levels.

If we have been in relationship with God from an early age, operating His method of dealing with our sin, we can enjoy freedom from accumulated sin and its consequences. If, however, we have chosen to store sin over several decades, and to build our inner structures on this, we must expect to reap the negative consequences of this. It would not be fair or consistent if God were simply to allow us to forget past sin, and suffer no consequences as a result.

Summing it up

The key factor in determining the extent of inner damage is not the degree to which we have been sinned against, but our reaction to that sin.

Wrong choices – made using our God-given free will – have opened us up for sin and its damaging potential to come home to roost within us. Making the right choices – as an act of that same sovereign free will – opens us up to the very power that will heal us.

Receiving healing, then, requires that we do two things. We must identify past and on-going sin in our make-up, and we must consciously give it up to God to take away.

This removes a barrier between us and God, and creates the space that He is looking for to allow Him to import more of Himself into us. We can then come to Him for His healing touch. The rest of the process of Christian healing is down to God, who will then have both the access to our damaged places, and the freedom to act that He has longed for.

God is always willing to provide us with all the help that we need to play our part in this process. However, no one else can actually carry it out for us.

Highlighting un-Christ-likeness in what we do and in what we are is the Holy Spirit's job. Showing us clearly all the ways in which we differ from Christ in our behaviour and in our inner make-up is something that only He can do. If we have made up our minds that this part of the process is either optional, or even dispensable, we will not be open to what He needs to show us. In this case, He will have to honour the choice that we are making to pay no attention to those parts of ourselves that need His light shining on them. The result will be that our healing process is, at least for the time being, held up.

The on-going exercise of forgiveness towards those that wrong us, and of repentance for our own sinful reactions, as well as learning to make godly choices in the first place, will keep us Christ-like and whole from now on. Where the wrong choices of the past are concerned, we will actively need to use the two clear-out tools that God has given us. Specifically, this means that **we will have to forgive those whose 'less-than-perfect-love' has contributed to our damaged state, and then to give God our un-Christ-like reactions**. This will make us receptive territory for the healing that God's Spirit longs to bring us.

The logic of Christian healing is simple enough. Our sins create a barrier between us and God, with His infinite power. They occupy our needy places and block them off from His healing love. We can exchange unforgiveness and other reactive sins of the past for wholeness and health in spirit, soul, mind, and body. The clear-out tools of forgiveness and repentance, that God has provided, give us all that we need to do this. In theory, nothing could be simpler. Yet the fact is that we woefully under-use both of these precious tools, which are not available at all to those outside Christ. As a result we experience only a fraction of the change that is available to us.

Taken in by an 'easy' Gospel

Having looked at what the Bible says we need to do to open the way for God to change us, we will begin, in the next chapter, to look at how we can apply this to our own lives. Before we do, however, we want to say a little more about why we think that so many Christians today are completely failing to do this, and at a time when there is otherwise so much openness to the supernatural work of God.

At any time that the people of God begin to truly surrender themselves to what He wants to do in and through them by His Spirit, Satan becomes seriously concerned. He works doubly hard to prevent the process going further – to keep closed the doors that God would want to see opening.

He knows our weaknesses, and lying is, as ever, his weapon.

Knowing that we are keen to win as many as possible to Christ, and naturally more comfortable bringing good news to our brothers and sisters, he has tempted many of the evangelists and teachers amongst us to distort the Gospel. 'Go light on sin,' he has said. 'God will take care of that. Emphasise the nice bits.' And we have fallen into his trap in a big way.

For some time now we have placed a strong emphasis on the giving nature of God. We have preached, quite rightly, that He loves us without reserve, and longs to shower blessing upon us. But instead of also reminding ourselves and others of **what Jesus said** about how we could get our hands on this blessing, we have often given the impression that asking is the key. The message has become: if we go on asking long enough, if we go to enough conferences and the like, His Holy Spirit will eventually come and give us what we want. The result is many people expending energy in the wrong direction.

Certainly God wants to know that we actually want what He has to offer. He cannot force anything on us, even if He knows it would be good for us, without first knowing that we want it too. But one sincere, specific request is more often than not enough for Him. This gives Him the permission He needs. In fact it would be quite inconsistent with His loving and giving nature for Him to hold back, simply to make us plead a little more and suffer a little longer.

Rather than encouraging one another to go on asking for blessings from a Father Christmas God, it would be much more valuable if we emphasised the place of sin, and the principle of relationship between us and our Creator. We are not robots controlled and changed unilaterally by God as He sees fit. We are individuals who have been given the right to choose what happens to us. This principle applies to inner transformation as much as to any other area of life.

In the areas where we are already whole, that wholeness will in itself have involved an element of our giving ourselves to God. We will have elected to give away self, and to become dwelling places for Him – though even here we could choose to 'repossess' ourselves at any time. In the same way, where ungodliness in any form still reigns within us, we must decide whether or not we want to surrender it to God.

This need to choose and to act applies to all of our being, including the deepest places. God, who very often respects and values our integrity, autonomy, and free will more than we do ourselves, will never, even if invited to do so, take us over wholesale. This is firstly because He can see the deeper places within us that may still want something else, and secondly because a wholesale takeover would end true relationship between two autonomous individuals – as He has designed it.

God's choice to relate to us, to have dialogue with us, and to influence us through relationship means, then, that we are given a very high and specific level of choice as regards all that we are. But, encouraged by the fast food mentality of our society that appeals to the natural laziness in all of us, we find the call to turn up, look up, and 'be blessed' – just like that – very appealing. The result of all this is that God's choice-respecting offers, expressed in phrases like *'repent, for the kingdom of heaven is at hand'*, are ignored, and our clear-out tools lie unused.

Free will – a precious gift

Some of us may have found this a challenging chapter. We may have been taught that supernatural change is something that we can pray for and just expect to happen to us. If this is so, and we are reluctant to let go of this idea, we should remember that there is another side to this particular coin. Unlike some of those powerful authority figures to whose imperfections we may have fallen victim in the past, God totally respects all that we are. He will neither infringe the free will that He has given us, nor force any change upon us – however good He may think it would be for us. Rather He has chosen to show us what we need to do for the best, and then to allow us to make our own decisions.

Add to this the fact that the part we have to play is actually very simple and small compared to the blessing that awaits us beyond it, and the need to participate takes on a different complexion.

We have ministered to a great many people over the years. Most of these have come to us with what have seemed to them insuperably large and complex barriers to Christ-like wholeness and radiance. Despite this, we have found that almost every one has been more than willing to do whatever was necessary. All that held them back was not knowing exactly what this was.

We have now completed our look at the main elements of the process of supernatural reconstruction. Keeping our eyes firmly on the prize that awaits us at the end of this process, we can now turn to the practicalities of actually putting God's clear-out tools to work in our own lives.

PART THREE

GIVING GOD ACCESS

Chapter 6

Connecting with the Healer

*'Jesus said, "Let **the little children** come to me..."'*
(Mark 10:14 NIV)

Children at heart

We saw in Chapter 3 that none of us receive our full share of God's truth-bearing love. This deprivation means that we do not grow up into Christ-like maturity and wholeness. We described the undernourished 'inner child' that lives on in all of us.

We also saw how, where the quality of nurture that we receive falls below God's perfect standard, what we called our 'justice and anger meters' will register this – the readings on both becoming cumulatively worse as time goes on. Made in the image of God, with souls that long for Him, we instinctively know when we are not receiving our full birthright.

The result is a continuing and increasing sense of deficit and anger. From deep within we complain and hanker after what we are owed.

This is only natural. But it presents Jesus with a problem. However willing He is to come by His Spirit, and to heal the deep, damaged places within each of us, what He almost invariably faces is illustrated in Figure 23.

On the surface, He may see an adult who is earnestly and expectantly looking to Him to make up what has been missed. But, deeper down, **in those parts of us where His**

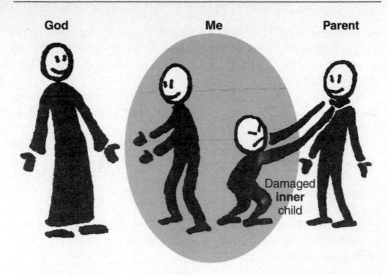

God   **Me**   **Parent**

Damaged
inner
child

Figure 23

healing presence is most needed, He encounters something quite different. There He finds a child looking angrily and insistently to the human beings of yesterday to 'pay up' what they owe. Rather than inviting Jesus in, this child is actually saying: 'Not now! I'm busy fighting a cold war with those who have let me down in the past. Go away!'

Under these circumstances there is nothing that Jesus can do but respect the free will of that child, who is a part of us, and wait.

The tool of forgiving

The drawing above represents chronic unforgiveness. But the tool of repentance will not release us from this sin. We need a different kind of tool to do this. This is because unforgiveness is a different kind of sin from all others.

All other sins are first and foremost offences against God. Unforgiveness, on the other hand, is a special kind of obstacle to the transforming work of the Holy Spirit. It is primarily something between ourselves and other people. **At the heart**

of unforgiveness is a choice to hold on to another sinfully. This is why confessing unforgiveness towards other people to God, and asking God's forgiveness, is not enough. **We** must forgive **them**, and let **them** go.

When we confess and repent of sins generally, **God** can then release us from their effect – namely the reaping, guilt, and punishment that comes with them. He can put us right with Him. **But where we harbour unforgiveness, we hold the solution in our own hands**. We have been sinned against. We alone can choose to release ourselves from being bound destructively, and to no useful purpose, to another.

To be freed from all other sins, we need God's forgiveness. To be freed from the binding effect of unforgiveness, **we must forgive**. God cannot pull the offender from our hurt and angry grasp.

As we have seen, only a supernatural injection of God's truth-bearing love can make up for what we have missed out on in the natural process of development. Holding on to human love sources in unforgiveness can, therefore, achieve nothing. It is a waste of time and effort.

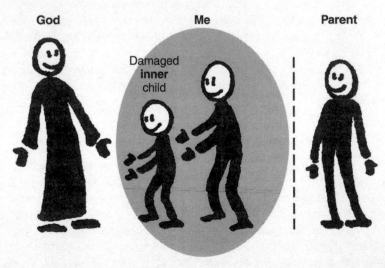

Figure 24

In view of this it is a wonder that we are often so slow to forgive. Perhaps poor teaching on forgiving is to blame. As soon as we do forgive, and let go of those who have failed us, the picture changes dramatically, as illustrated in Figure 24.

Forgiving enables us to **'disconnect' ourselves** from those who have failed us in the past, and to connect with God in those deep parts of us that need His touch. In doing this we take a giant step towards the healing that He longs to bring us.

This is the crux of forgiving. But there is more that we need to know about it than just this. Because understanding forgiving properly, and doing it, is so important, we have devoted the whole of Part Three to this subject. At this point, however, we want just to add that **it is possible to forgive entirely effectively without having to speak it out, face to face, to those who need our forgiveness.**

Chapter 7

Letting Go

Evaluating our formative years

Once we have grasped the crucial importance of forgiving to our own healing process, the next thing we need to do is to establish who we still need to forgive, and what for.

Many of us may be aware of carrying a mixture of negative feelings and memories about the past. We may even be able to link these to specific relationships and events. But few, if any of us, will have a clear and comprehensive overview of how our upbringing missed God's ideal for us.

By and large our own families are all that we know. However abnormal they may actually have been, compared with other families, to a large extent we accept what happened in them as the norm. We were immersed in them. We did not have a bird's-eye view.

Because of this, we need an objective yardstick to assess our own experience by. We need some hard facts to attach to the general feelings generated by the readings on our 'justice and anger meters'. We need an authoritative guide to show us exactly who we need to forgive and what for.

God is more than willing to provide this. In the same way that He can convict us of our own sin, He can also show us the sin of others against us. The purpose of this chapter is to be part of that process of illumination.

What are the elements of the truth-bearing love that God wants us to be given during our formative years? How, in practical terms, does He intend this love to be brought home to us?

The purpose of the guide that follows is to answer these questions. It is set out just as God gave it to us – as if He were personally instructing parents and other nurturers.

We have presented this countless times to those we have counselled. It has been the key that has unlocked the door to dramatic change in many lives. Expressed in this way, it seems to have a particular power – not only to enlighten, but also to comfort.

For many of us, realising the extent to which we have been let down can be profoundly upsetting. We often build our lives on a pretence that all was well. We try to bury uncomfortable truths about our past family relationships. Being brought face to face with those truths can temporarily create a painful vacuum. Hearing what God in His love wanted for us all along, as if it were from His own mouth, can begin to fill that vacuum straight away.

The Psalmist reminds us that:

> *'Although my father and my mother have forsaken me, yet the Lord will take me up [adopt me as His child].'*
>
> (Psalm 27:10)

Our guide is in the form of a message, supplemented with explanations and diagrams, that reveals God's heart to prospective parents and other nurturers. Conveyed like this, the Holy Spirit has used it to do two things: to show people the full extent to which their parents and others have failed them, and so need to be forgiven, and, at the same time, to bring them healing and restoring truth about God their Father, and the quality of His everlasting love.

God's pre-natal brief to parents and other nurturers

The overall objective

I am God. I am love, and I am endlessly creative. I care for everything that I make. Of everything that I have created, people are the jewel in my crown. This is because I have made them like me in so many ways. This means that we can understand one another, and have a relationship.

One of the most important characteristics that we have in common is this creative and caring nature. That is why, beginning with two people coming together in love, and with what you call 'conception', I have made it possible for them to share with me, even in my greatest work of creation – that of bringing a person into existence, and then nurturing him to full maturity.

I am **the** Creator. I instigate and mastermind the creation and nurture of every human-being. I am in and behind every aspect of this creative process, but have chosen to share it by delegating parts of it to the people I have created. I **could** accomplish every aspect of the creation of a fully mature human being on my own. Some parts of this process I do perform sovereignly and exclusively. For example, I give people no hand in the mechanics of actually putting together the biological basics of each human being. It is I, also, who place a human spirit within each person. Even the aspects of creation that I do share with people need my help, if they are to be carried out properly. I set the limits to people's ability to understand and to be safely involved in this aspect of my Creation. I ask no one to go beyond these.

In this area of my creative activity, as in many others, people and I are partners. I am the senior partner, and they the junior. I am in overall control, and ask them to do only what is necessary to fulfil their creative natures, and is within the limits of the ability that I have set within them.

However, the part they have been given to play is a vital one. It is not just a game, but has real consequences in the lives of those I am creating. If this were not so then I wouldn't really be sharing my work of creation at all, or the wonderful and deep sense of fulfilment that there is in bringing it to completion.

This, as many millions of people, and especially parents, know, is a deeply fulfilling experience, but when it goes wrong this has very real consequences in the young life concerned – consequences that can last a lifetime. For this reason, I have always made available the most detailed instructions on how this work of creation should be carried out. I have done this both by my written Word and by my Spirit. If people listen to my instructions and follow them, the result will be a whole, mature, happy, and satisfied life.

You have decided, in the context of your love for me and for each other, that you want to share with me in this area of my creative work. I want to give you this privilege and pleasure, so I have set the creative process in motion through you and given you a child.

This is **my child**. Beginning with caring for him in the womb and praying for him, I want you to help me with the wonderful work of bringing him into the world. Then, while enjoying him for the special, unique individual that he is, I want you to help me with the process of bringing him to full maturity, and of seeing that he finds and fulfils the unique calling in life that I already have in mind for him. This will bring about my purpose for him and ensure him the best possible life.

It is my wish that this child, when he becomes a young adult, will be ready to leave home, and to fully and effectively take charge of his own life under me. I want him, therefore, to go out with a deep and accurate know-ledge of who I am and what I am like. In particular, I want him to know that I am always with him, as God and as a friend, and that I love him unconditionally all the time. I also want him to go enabled to relate to me and to his fellow creatures fully in love. This is because I create everyone primarily for relationship with me, and then, secondarily, for relationship with other people.

Like all children, this child will be a unique individual with free will. Like all children, with the exception of Jesus himself, he will not start life with his own relationship with me. The only way that he will be able to experience me and my kind of love, and be prepared for a living relationship with me, will be through his contact with you, with significant others, and with my Creation. What I want is for you to 'be me', and to bring my kind of love to this child. I want you to point him towards me in such a way that, as well as always having experienced me (through you and your example), he will quite naturally and freely choose to come into his own relationship with me – fully enabled for this and other relationships generally.

In this way we can together ensure that, although he has his own free will and will have to make his own choice to have direct relationship with me, in a sense I will never not have been there for him.

Ephesians 6:1 conveys this idea of parents being God's agents. It says in the Amplified Version:

> 'Children, obey your parents in the Lord [**as His representatives**], for this is just and right.'

A diagram (Figure 25) will help us to summarise this first part of the brief.

From the very first moments of our existence we are God's property. We belong to Him, and He takes primary responsibility for our lives.

He does not hand us over to our parents lock, stock, and barrel. He simply asks them to play a part, under Him, in raising us and bringing about His plans for our lives.

It is as if we are on temporary loan to them, until the age of about eighteen – to be nurtured and enjoyed. When that time comes, God wants us to have been equipped to leave home and take charge of our own lives under Him.

In the meantime, God has four main objectives. In order that we will be prepared for the richest possible quality of life, He wants us to be:

1. filled with His truth-bearing love;
2. deeply aware of His existence, and what He is like;
3. fully the people He made us to be;
4. pointing in the direction of His plan for our lives.

Putting it another way, He wants the longings that He has placed in our souls to be fully satisfied.

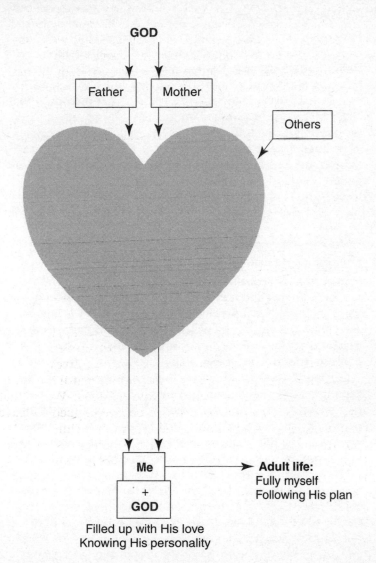

Figure 25

An agenda in two parts

Now, in order to 'be me' to this child, and to show him my kind of love, you will need to do two things in parallel – a sort of **double agenda**. Though both parts of the agenda are for all parents to apply to all children, the first part is **specific** to this child, because it has to do with the things about this child which are unique and make him like no other. The second part is **general**, because it has to do with needs that all children have in common.

If we build this into our diagram (Figure 25), it becomes as shown in the diagram on the next page (Figure 26).

The specific agenda

I am intimately acquainted with every person I create.

It is I who give them their bodies, souls, and spirits. I give them their individual personalities and gifts. Each is unique, and I know the purpose for which I have created them. I know exactly what nurture each one needs to perfectly fulfil that purpose, and so to most fully enjoy the life that I give them.

My specific agenda for you is that, with one eye and one ear on me, and one eye and one ear on the child, you should get to know him. I want you, with my help, to pinpoint the personality and the special gifts that I have given him. I then want you to affirm that personality and to encourage those gifts. Finally, I want you to lead him out into his life-calling.

I have a plan for this child's life. I want you to help him to find and to fulfil that plan. Your job is to discover what this child is all about, and to get under and behind that, no matter what it is. There will be others who help you in this, but you have overall responsibility to enable him to know and to grow in his own particular personality and gifting, and so, ultimately, to be his own Christ-like self in, and to, the world.

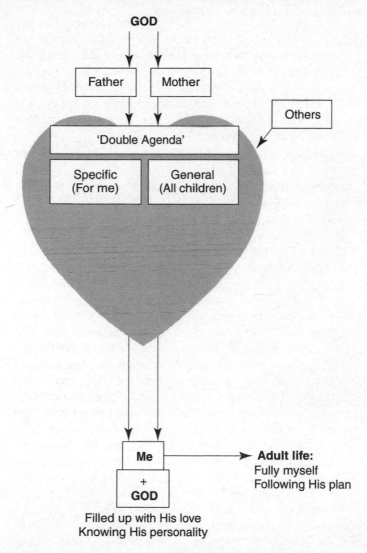

Figure 26

If we build this into our diagram (Figure 25) as well, it becomes as shown below (Figure 27).

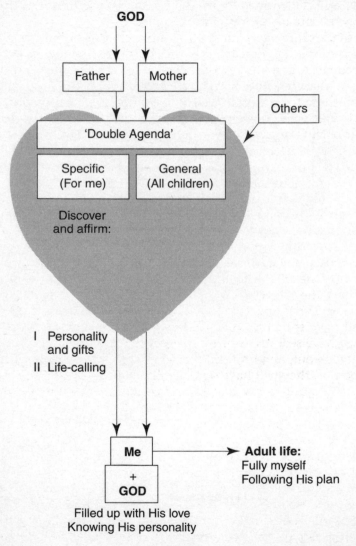

Figure 27

A child is to a mature adult what a seed is to a plant. A seed contains all the essential ingredients of that plant. Though initially invisible to the naked eye, those ingredients will, if the seed is identified for what it is and cultivated in the right way, eventually grow up into the plant.

In the same way, contained within each of us as children are all the essential ingredients of the adult that God means us to become. A parent's responsibility is to identify the kind of 'seed' that they have been given, and to supply the right kind of nurture to grow that 'seed' into a blooming, healthy plant.

Unlike seeds, however, we do not come in packets that tell our parents in advance precisely what type we are. We arrive with no label around our necks detailing the exact conditions and nutrients that we need to enable us to become fully ourselves. These things parents and others must get to know in the only way that any one human being can get to know another – through the process of relationship, dialogue, and observation. They also need information from the Maker.

Discovering with delight, over the years, exactly what they have been given in each of the children that God lends them, is just one of the joys that God has destined for parents. Where they have worked with God to discover all that we are, and to bring **His** plans for our lives to fruition, they will have stored up much blessing for us. Where, however, they have seen us as being more or less their own property, left God out, and imposed their own aspirations for our lives upon us, they will have significantly denied us this.

This is not to say that where parents are not themselves Christians, and have, therefore, no direct relationship of their own with God, they must necessarily have been unable to hear God and to carry out His agenda for us at all. Nor is it to suggest that where they do know God personally, they will necessarily have fulfilled it anywhere near perfectly.

This is because how well our parents will have done depends also on how whole and Christ-like they are. This, in turn, will be influenced by the state of **their parents'** relationship with God, and on how whole, Christ-like, and able to hear God they were. Whether they can truly empathise with, affirm, and encourage their children depends as much on a parent's having received these things themselves as it does on their simply being 'born again'.

We see the impact of one truly and deeply Christian life on the generational flow of parenting in this way: it is like a stone thrown into a pond. This first creates a splash, and then ever-widening and ever-diminishing ripples. In terms of its impact on many generations of doing things the worldly way, a truly Christian life is like the splash on the surface of the pond. It introduces the things of God in a radical way, and generates ripples that run on long after the splash has gone.

For each subsequent generation that a family remains truly Christian, the power of that splash continues undiminished. It is as if there were one perpetual splash. However, even when the chain of true Christianity is broken in a family, the ripples continue down the generations. Though they are ever-diminishing as the non-Christian generations go by, the ripples continue to be felt in the nurturing process of each generation. Nothing matches a direct relationship with God, especially when accompanied by deep inner transformation. But, even without this, each generation of children nonetheless passes on a large measure of the good that it receives to its own children.

Against the background of these general principles, some common examples of parents departing from this aspect of God's Agenda are:

1. Parents imposing their own personality, interests, tastes, and religious beliefs on their children.

2. Parents trying to live out their own failed aspirations through their children.

3. Parents considering a particular calling or career (or marriage) not to be good enough for their children for social reasons.

4. Parents placing too much importance on money as a source of security and well-being for their children, with the effect that what are seen as financially insecure callings are ruled out.

5. Parents forcefully grooming their children to run a family business.

As we have seen, this first part of God's 'Double Agenda' for parents caters for the unique aspects of every child. If there is one scripture that sums it up, it is this:

> *'Train up a child in the way **he should go** [and **in keeping with his individual gift or bent**], and when he is old he will not depart from it.'* (Proverbs 22:6)

We now move on to the second part of the Agenda, which is designed to fulfil the needs for truth-bearing love that the souls of all children have in common.

The general agenda

My general agenda for every child is this: you must love him **in the way that I do** at all times.

You must do this quite irrespective of what he does or fails to do, and of whether this pleases you personally or not. You must also **show him** at all times that you love him.

This means two distinct things. First, you must have love for him in your head and your heart. Second, you must outwardly demonstrate this love.

It is, of course, important that you have feelings of love for him inside you, but, to the extent that you do not communicate that love, it is wasted and cannot bless the child.

There are four interdependent ways to fully and effectively communicate love as I understand it to a child.

1. Words

You must be sure to **tell** the child in different ways that you love him unconditionally. Do this constantly to begin with. Later on you can tell him less frequently – just when the original message seems to need underlining.

Nothing can adequately substitute for telling a child that you love him.

Saying 'I love you' defines the relationship in a way in which nothing else can.

The example of adult courtship will help us to illustrate what we mean here.

There is always a progression between a couple's first meeting with one another and their getting married. Conventionally it goes something like this: they meet; they are mutually attracted; they begin to get to know one another; they date regularly; they become engaged to be married; and, finally, they marry.

It would be an unusual relationship in which neither one of the couple ever, in this progression, told the other that they loved them. It is, indeed, difficult to see how such a couple could easily make it to the altar. Why? Because a relationship like this needs defining. Both parties need to know its exact nature. This, in turn, means each knowing not only how they feel about the other person, but also how the other person feels about them.

'Tell me you love me!' has been the impassioned cry of many a hero or heroine in romantic movies down the years. It exemplifies the overwhelming, almost all-consuming need that each of us has to hear the one we love say that they feel the same way about us. They can give us clues – they can meet with us constantly; they can compliment us; they can hug us; they can kiss us; they can buy us gifts; they can empathise with us; they can have everything in common with us – but if they never tell us that they love us, we lack the defining and most important piece of the jigsaw puzzle.

It is the same with children. They need to be told that they are loved – and repeatedly. It takes time for them to thoroughly absorb this message, and they have an Enemy who is constantly trying to use both people and situations that arise to tell them something quite different.

There are, of course, many different ways of saying 'I love you'. What is important is that parents and other nurturers convey a message that expresses the same kind of love as God has for people – that is to say, a love that is unconditional, and independent of anything that children might do – a love that values them for who they are.

'Well done', for example, does not count at all here. There is an important place for parents affirming a child's personality and gifts by showing that they **share in its joy** at some form of personal progress or achievement. However, repeatedly praising success or good behaviour can convey a love that is conditional. Words like 'Well done' can say: 'Love is something that is there for you when you do well in my eyes, but not otherwise.' Rather than freeing a child to be themselves, they bind it to forever trying to please others for 'love'. This is all the more the case when a parent's 'Well done' actually means: 'What you have done has suited my convenience.'

The only kind of 'Well done' that is acceptable here is: 'Well done ... for simply being you.'

In one family that we know, the parents habitually call all their children 'treasure'. We cannot think of a better expression of unconditional love for a child than this.

2. Actions

You must also express your love for the child through actions. These must range from affectionate embraces to loving actions of a more practical kind.

Touch and bodily warmth are crucial channels of nurture. As with words, physical expressions of affection should be constant and repeated to begin with. Remember, the child's experience in the womb will have been one of constant physical contact with a parent, and the deep need for touch still remains very strong after birth.

As the child grows and his independence increases, he will give you clear signals that he needs less physical touch and affection. However, though less frequent, regular expressions of affection, like kisses and hugs, should continue throughout the length of the relationship.

The more practical actions that I have in mind are those that show empathy and care by meeting or anticipating the child's other day-to-day needs.

We are much more than mere intellect. We were designed to receive the truth-bearing love that our souls crave through all of our senses, including touch. For example, when, as babies, we feed at our mother's breast, we are drinking in far more than just our mother's milk. This skin-to-skin experience is feeding our souls with a sense of acceptance, security, and more.

Especially in the earliest months and years, it will often have been parents who initiated loving touch. However, it is just as important that they should have been able to read and respond adequately to signals of need from us – for example our outstretched arms, or sometimes our tears – that said: 'Please hold me.'

What we see, too, plays an important part in the quality of love that actually comes home to us.

Smiling faces spell unconditional love and acceptance. Frowning or angry faces mean a love source that needs placating in some way before it will 'love' us. It does not matter that the anger may have nothing to do with us. Unless it is made clear to us that the anger has other roots (and, where those roots are deep, it rarely is) then we assume that it has to do with the way we are, or with something we have said or done.

3. Time

You must spend time with the child. Your just being near him will bless him and feed his soul in many ways. However, only regular times spent focused exclusively on him, letting him set the agenda and entering into his world, will fully satisfy this part of my plan.

The main focus of this part of God's 'General Agenda' is that we should grow up knowing:

1. That God is a friend.
2. That He really likes our company.
3. That He is interested in the things that interest and affect us.
4. That He can truly enter, and understand, our world.

Whilst the longing that we have to be with our parents, and to have their attention, is to some degree met by our just being near them, this alone is not enough. They need to do more than ask us to 'help' them whilst they fix the car, do the housework and shop, or pursue special interests of their own. They must get involved with us in the things that **we personally like doing** at the different stages of our growing up. They need to play **our games** with us, as **we** set the agenda.

Linda was badly failed in this area. Given the other pressures on them, her parents' time was taken up elsewhere. Not until God came supernaturally to the little girl, in a perfect demonstration of how this part of the 'Double Agenda' should be carried out, did she receive the message that He, or indeed anyone, really liked her and understood her needs. Until then a sense of isolation had filled her soul.

4. Knowing and understanding

It is your job to get to know and to understand this child – how he thinks and how he feels. Expressions of love must be accurately targeted if they are to fully bless him. They will not be if you cannot 'read' him and so know his needs at any given time.

We have heard it said that love is 'an accurate measure and supply of another's needs'. We think that this is as good a definition of love as any we have heard.

Under the 'General Agenda', we have broken the ingredients that go to make up essential food for nurture in every human life into four separate parts. In reality, however, these parts overlap. Together they fulfil this objective: that a child should be really known, and its true needs, as God sees them, supplied at all times.

Amongst these needs (though children will not always immediately see it this way!) is the need for discipline. They are to be reared *'[tenderly] in the training and discipline and the counsel and admonishment of the Lord'* (Ephesians 6:4). Loving control is to be applied where it is called for.

Figure 28 shows how God's 'Double Agenda' looks with all its elements in place.

Although we have also expressed them separately, in reality the 'Specific and General Agendas', too, are inextricably linked – hence the broken arrow from right to left towards the bottom of this last diagram.

As our parents spend time with us – playing with us, watching us, and having dialogue with us; as they come to really know and understand how we tick and how we feel, so they are able to truly discover our personalities and gifts, to affirm them, and to help us to find our life-calling.

The 'Double Agenda' and other nurturers

In God's order of things, it is our natural parents that are His main agents for giving us what we need to come to full, Christ-like maturity. However, there are a whole range of other people that are called to contribute to this process.

First and foremost amongst these will be our grandparents, aunts and uncles, godparents, close friends of our parents, baby-sitters, child-minders, and teachers at school.

These will be followed by our contemporaries – like brothers and sisters, children of our godparents and of our parents' close friends, as well as our school-mates. (People in this group are all, in a sense, still in training to reflect God to others. Nevertheless they can begin to do so, under adult guidance, from the word go.)

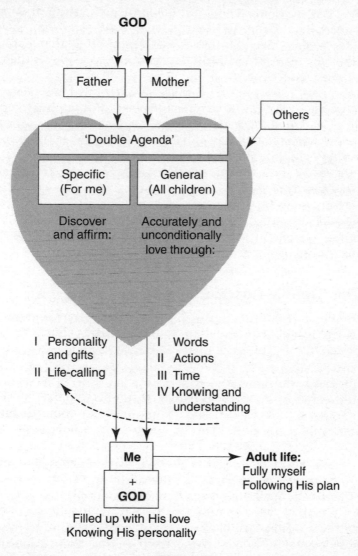

Figure 28

Lastly, this secondary category may include one or more of God's 'mavericks'. These are people who unusual circumstances may put into a position where they can significantly love, protect, or guide us as children. They may be people who are in a formal relationship with us – like adoptive parents, step-parents, or social workers – or they may be people in a less formal relationship with us. Anyone, from next-door neighbours to people we meet only once – for example, on our first journey alone, or when we become lost in a public place – may come into this category.

God's brief to all these people is that they should recognise, respect, and support our parents in their role of reflecting God's nature and conveying His love to us. He calls them all, in differing degrees, to play their part in the process of forming our souls. The greater the involvement a person has in our lives the greater their responsibility under the 'Double Agenda'.

The 'Double Agenda' and absent nurturers

In most cases, the process of disconnecting from those who have harmed us is all about evaluating what God's designated nurturers actually did, and then comparing it with God's perfect standard. Usually we are dealing with nurturers who were there, but simply fell short of perfection in their efforts to carry out God's instructions.

Sometimes, however, one or more of our key nurturers were not there at all. This is increasingly the case in our divorce-ridden society.

There are many negative feelings that the absence of a key nurturer can generate as between us and God – particularly where such absence is brought about by their dying early. Suffice it to say here that God is invariably given the role of a dustbin for blame for which we can find no other obvious target. However, the truth is that their departure is never the result of some malign plan of God's. Rather it is always the result of human sin, and sometimes, in the case of premature death, the sickness that flows from this. If we allow Him to, God has the power to turn every event to good, no matter how devastating it may have been in the past.

It is important to evaluate every absent nurturer (especially a natural parent), who ceased to play a part in our nurture in the way that God intended, against all the elements of the 'Double Agenda'. They may fail on every count, but **it is vital that we do not gloss over any detail of what their absence has meant**.

Most children see the departure of one parent from the family home as a specific rejection of themselves. It may be that relations between a parent and a given child were already poor before they left the home. Even in these circumstances, however, the child's line of reasoning, which is hard to argue with, will usually have been: 'No matter what the situation between you and (mummy/daddy), if you **really loved me** you wouldn't have left **me**.'

Another common result of the breakdown of marriages is that children are left endlessly wondering whether it was something wrong with them that caused the absent parent to leave.

These are some of the special considerations that we need to take into account where one or more of our own key nurturers were absent.

Why it is so important that we evaluate our past and forgive

Every shortfall in the carrying out of God's perfect plan for our development damages us in some way or other. Every failure of those with a nurturing responsibility towards us to apply God's 'Double Agenda' needs, without exception, to be acknowledged by us, and forgiven. None is truly dealt with by our simply ignoring it, or trying to forget about it in an effort to 'move on'.

Whilst our own fallen natures, with their self-deceiving defence mechanisms, often cause us to avoid or to play down uncomfortable truths, God sees our pasts through pure and clear eyes. He knows precisely what each of our nurturers should have done, and what it will mean if they have not.

Something God said to me (Richard) recently highlights the contrast that often exists between our perspective and His, where the content of our formative years is concerned.

It is a sad fact that helping victims of childhood sexual abuse, often committed by parents, is now a routine part of our ministry. Against the background of this experience, which I know we share with many others in the Christian healing ministry, I was asking God to show me more about His view of how children should be loved.

'Richard,' He said, 'to love is to bring Jesus in His entirety to another person.

You use the word 'abuse' to describe maltreatment of children of a particularly unpleasant and damaging kind. As I see it, simply not to cherish a child with all your heart is to abuse and maltreat it.'

This brief exchange reminded me how important it is that we are open to fresh perspectives from God on our own past. If we want to experience the kind of far-reaching inner reconstruction that is our birthright as Christians, we need to listen carefully to Him. We must allow Him to tell us what does and does not need to be taken seriously. We need to let Him show us, **from His perspective**, the things that we must first of all specifically acknowledge as shortfalls in our own upbringings, and then forgive. If we do not, we will forever be held to the damage of the past. We will, for reasons we touched on in the previous chapter, be closed to the healing touch of God in our deepest places.

Postscript – a word of warning to parents

We are only too conscious that for each person who reads this chapter, and becomes aware of the shortcomings of God's human agents towards them, there is just as likely to be another who becomes aware of their own shortcomings as an agent of God's truth-bearing love to others.

It is neither our intention nor God's that any parent or other agent should be made to feel condemned for their mistakes by what they have learned in this chapter. It is not His desire to condemn any of us, but to make us whole. What He does want to do is to help us to pinpoint who **we** need to forgive and what for. It is important that we keep our eyes firmly on this goal.

That said, an awareness of our own shortcomings as nurturers, far from being a hindrance to our own healing walks, can actually help us.

Children absorb much more of what their parents **are** than they do of what those parents try to teach them. If, for example, parents are worriers then children will grow up to be worriers too. Being told not to worry will not override this. This means that what I am like, including the mistakes I make as a parent, is a replica of what my parents were like, including the mistakes they made with me. Seen in this light, an awareness of our failures as parents actually helps to highlight the things that we need to forgive our own parents for.

As far as any damage to our children that has resulted is concerned, we need to remember that, if we commit them to Him, it is God who is in charge of their lives – including their healing. They are His responsibility. It is not for us to go rushing off and trying to put all our mistakes and any resulting damage right overnight. Our responsibility is to concentrate on letting God make **us** more Christ-like. We will then automatically – just by being our new selves – become an active ingredient in His healing prescription for the lives of those around us.

If our children are still with us in the home, then becoming aware of our mistakes as nurturers will mean that we can do things better from now on. If we need to make any specific apology for the past, God will show us by providing glaring opportunities for this, and making it clear at the time what needs to be said.

Chapter 8

Five Common Barriers
to Truly Letting Go

We may accept that letting go of nurturers who have failed us is crucial to allowing God to make us whole. We may also have a good idea of who we need to forgive, and what we need to forgive them for. Yet we may still fail to do this effectively.

Only true and unreserved forgiveness disconnects the little boy or girl inside us from those who have let us down, and opens our souls to the healing work of the Holy Spirit. So, because forgiving properly is of such vital importance, and because it is a bridge that, sadly, few ever cross, we now want to look at some further common barriers to truly letting go.

In our experience, there are five such barriers:

1. We do not understand what forgiving asks of us.
2. We believe that to acknowledge our parents' imperfec-
    tions is to dishonour them.
3. We think that denying what we really feel will serve us
    better.
4. We are afraid that we may become orphans.
5. We forgive too quickly.

Any one of these barriers can prevent our forgiving in the way that we need to, and so bar our way to transformation. Because of this, we devote this chapter to dismantling them.

1. Misunderstanding forgiveness

Many think that to forgive is to do one or more of the following:

1.   To pretend that what an offender has done to us has not really mattered.
2.   To grit our teeth and to think positively about an offender and what we have suffered, because this will help us to feel better, and because God likes us always to be thinking only nice thoughts about everyone.
3.   To provide an excuse for an offender by 'understanding' their shortcomings, and the pressures on them at the time.
4.   To somehow suppress any sense we have that an offender ought to be brought to justice.

To look at forgiving in these terms is to miss the point of it entirely. In particular, it is to see it as something that we do primarily for God and for other people.

True forgiving is actually **none** of these things.

Others do indeed benefit from receiving our forgiveness, but it is first and foremost something that is good **for us**.

The words 'I forgive' are not some kind of magic formula that we can trot out mindlessly. If we are to be released into a place where we can receive God's healing, we must **truly forgive**, in God's sense of the word. Because of this, we must make sure that, when we are doing what we think is forgiving, we are not in fact doing something quite different.

One of the most common mistakes that people make is to think that to forgive is simply to understand an offender's shortcomings, and in this way to become 'friends' with them again.

Although this response to being wronged seems noble, it is essentially a way of running away from bad experiences and the pain and loss that they cause us. By focusing our attention on the offender, trying to see things from their point of view, and going to their side, we fly from acknowledging our own pain. 'We have no right to place blame at their door,' we tell ourselves. 'They were only doing their best. In their position, we would probably have done the same.'

Forgiveness **is not** excusing another by coming to understand why they did what they did. This may help us to forgive them, but it is not forgiveness in itself. It is actually avoiding true forgiving, and in particular the discomfort involved in acknowledging what an offender has really done to us.

This approach to being wronged has another attraction. If we can make excuses for the sins of others against us, we can do the same for our own sins against them. If we really acknowledge the truth about the effect of the sins of others against us, then inevitably we will have to acknowledge the full enormity of our own against them. Given this, it often suits us to become part of a culture of 'understanding', rather than one of true forgiving.

'Understanding' the sins of others against us frequently goes hand in hand with low self-esteem. This is often mistaken for humility. As a result we think: 'Who am I, a sinner, to accuse anyone else of wrongdoing?'

This approach can also flow from confusion about the commandment not to judge others. We are not to play God, or to condemn, but this does not mean that we can never see the sins of others against us for what they are. If this were so, how would we ever be in a position to forgive anyone?

As adults we can sometimes understand and rationalise the behaviour of others as an aid to forgiving them. We can sometimes even use understanding to avoid being hurt at all in the first place. However, to try to rationalise away the hurts we have already received as children, is like closing the proverbial stable door after the horse has bolted. It is like trying to raise a shield long after we have been wounded by an arrow.

Rationalisation is always a glossing over of part of the truth. It cuts the wounded parts of us off from God's healing. It says to them: 'Be quiet! You have no place to complain. Put yourself in the offender's shoes and understand them. Isn't that what you would want them to do if you hurt them?'

When we are children we need the nurture that God prescribes. Nothing else will do. It is as crucial to our growing up whole as the air that we breathe is to our physical existence. Were God to decide, mistakenly, to turn off the world's oxygen supply tomorrow, simply to try to understand His reasons for doing this would not help us a great deal! Finding an explanation, some years after the event, for what made Him think this was necessary would be equally unsatisfactory! Yet this is exactly the kind of exercise we engage in when we rationalise the sins of those who nurtured us. It may keep a kind of peace, but it does nothing to move the damaged little boy or girl inside us forward.

Another common tendency is to imagine that forgiving means suppressing any sense of injustice that the failures of nurturers have generated within us. This also could not be further from the truth. To forgive is not to suppress our sense of injustice, but to see that it is actually satisfied in the most effective way possible – by putting the case into God's hands. When we forgive we actually hand an offender and all their offences against us over to God, and say: 'Here you are, Lord. You be judge and jury. You fix and carry out the sentence. Thank you that, when You say, *"It is mine to avenge; I will repay"* (Deuteronomy 32:35 NIV), I can depend on You completely to see that justice is done on my behalf.'

To truly forgive one who has offended against us is to say:

> 'You **have** wronged me. This is what you have done, and this is exactly what I feel about it. It has harmed me. It does matter. But I want **to release myself** from you, and to **hand you over** to God, with full confidence that He will restore me and, on my behalf, will confront you with the truth and see that justice is fully and fairly done. I am unburdening myself of you and the things that you have done to me, and relinquishing all claims on you, so that I can focus myself entirely on Jesus and the healing that He longs to bring me.'

2. Forgiveness and honouring our parents

As we have seen, the delicate mechanism that makes up a human being was designed to be nurtured in an atmosphere of perfect love and complete sinlessness. Anything short of this will have damaged and distorted the people that we were meant to be, as our spirits have reacted to it and our souls absorbed it.

As we have also seen, God gives particular people an important share of the active responsibility for providing this atmosphere. Foremost amongst these are our parents.

The closer they are to God, and the more perfectly they represent Him, the better they can enable us, in every respect, to reach our full, God-given potential. Unfortunately, because of the position of power and responsibility that they hold, the reverse is also true. **They have the capacity to contribute more deeply and widely than anyone else to un-Christ-likeness within us**. The further they are from God, and the less able they are to reflect Him and minister His quality of love to us, the more they will have held us back.

What all this means is that, when we look at those who we might need to forgive, it is those who have been closest to us whose role in our lives we must examine most carefully. This is true even where, at first glance, it seems to be other people that have done us most harm.

It may be, for example, that damage that has come to us through relationships of our own choosing actually has its real origins in the failures of our primary nurturers towards us. They may have failed in their duty to equip us to relate wisely and constructively to others. It may be their failure to protect us that was the reason we had contact with those others in the first place.

Amongst the most common and far-reaching causes of damage today is serial promiscuity. This is driven most commonly by an insatiable craving to feel truly loved in the deep places of our being. We can only guess at how many millions of ultimately destructive relationships have had at their root an attempt by both partners to make up deficits in love and affirmation that were created by shortcomings in parental love in childhood and teenage years.

As parties to such relationships go from one partner to another, giving their all and being repeatedly hurt as they try in vain to collect their birthright – a sense of being valued and loved simply for who they are – who needs their forgiveness most? Is it those who, in their own search for precisely that same sense of self-worth, fail to provide what it is now too late for any human agent to impart to them? Or is it those who failed, in the God-given order of things, to write this sense of self-worth deep within them in the first place?

However obvious the consequences of their failures, there is very often still a deep reluctance in those we counsel to properly acknowledge the shortcomings of their parents. This is because they are afraid that to do this would be to dishonour them. They are concerned, as Christians, not to break the Fifth Commandment.

This concern is unfounded and springs from a failure to understand what honouring really means.

To honour means to highly respect. When God tells us to honour our parents, He is essentially asking us to do two things. Firstly, as in the case of all our relationships, we are to love them *'warmly'* from the heart. This is Jesus' Second Commandment (Matthew 22:39), amplified by Peter (1 Peter 1:22 LB), and it includes speaking about them to others in a way that we would want to be spoken about ourselves. Over and above this, however, we are to give them a special respect in their role as our parents. We are to honour them in the sense of being thankful for them, following their example, and obeying them.

The first thing that needs to be said is that none of this in any way prevents us, as children, questioning our parents' decisions and actions. The requirement that children follow their parents' leading is itself based on the assumption that those parents are, in turn, following God's instructions on how children should be brought up. There is a basic presumption that our parents almost always know best. At the end of the day we must do as they say. But this in no way precludes us from subjecting them, respectfully, to the same scrutiny as anyone else.

Good parents will ensure that their children – who, after all, are just little people, with valid views and feelings of their own – expressly understand that they are free to question and complain. They will allow discussion of their decisions. It may be that some are too insecure or too proud to allow themselves to be 'criticised' in this way. Others may fear a loss of the control that an illusion of infallibility gives them. But no parents are perfect. So not to allow a child to raise questions in this way is to fuel the fires of a volcano. Even if this does not one day erupt, the damage to the child's spiritual, emotional, and physical health will already have been done.

Even when we are children then, God's requirement that we honour our parents does not mean that we must behave as if they are perfect. Once we reach adulthood, however, and 'leave' our natural family, the obeying aspect of our responsibility to honour our parents also falls away. Parents' work as instructors is done, and the relationship becomes one of a dialogue between adults. We should by then have become our own people – entitled to weigh, to agree or disagree with, and ultimately to decide to accept or reject the advice and opinions of our parents. Young children do not have the wisdom or knowledge to know what proper parenting is all about. They cannot assess their parents as parents. By the time they are grown-up, the position is quite different.

If we see the duty to honour in these terms, it is clear that the process of openly acknowledging our parents' shortcomings as parents, so that we can meaningfully and comprehensively forgive them, in no way conflicts with our God-given responsibility to honour them. Rather, doing this will in fact enable us to better fulfil this responsibility. The inner healing process – of which forgiving those who have sinned against us is such an indispensable part – will always enhance our ability to love others generally. But potentially the greatest beneficiaries are our parents and others close to us.

To summarise, we need have no concern about making a methodical, open-minded, and comprehensive assessment of our parents' performance, and expressing what we truly feel about this. This is because:

1. Healing will enhance our ability to truly love them from the heart, and to respect them as fellow human beings.

2. We cannot receive that healing without first forgiving them, and we cannot do this properly without working out precisely how they have failed us.

3. Our motive for focusing on their shortcomings is not to dishonour them, but to pursue greater Christ-likeness within ourselves and in all our relationships, including with them.

4. The only others who need be part of this process are *bona fide* counsellors. They will be concerned neither to judge our parents, nor to broadcast their shortcomings. They will simply want to help us in our own process of healing.

3. Denying the hurt

Each time we are inwardly wounded, we have two options. We can either live endlessly in the memories and the pain that result, or we can try to somehow switch them off. Only the Holy Spirit can really heal, and so draw out pain once and for all. Unlike Jesus, however, we do not always know about this route to recovery, or how to apply it to our own lives. Instead we have our own ways of finding relief.

Our fallen nature means that we are often more concerned with getting rid of immediate discomfort than with true inner Christ-likeness. As a result we commonly opt for a form of 'mind over matter': denial.

To deny something is to refuse to recognise it, to disown it, or to declare it untrue. We may do any or all of these things with bad memories and the painful feelings that go with them. In this way, we try to neutralise their unpleasant consequences, by pushing them out of our conscious mind and out of the realm of our feelings. We make them go away by pretending that they simply are not there.

Linda did this. 'It wasn't until I reached my thirties that I admitted to myself that my childhood had been anything less than perfect,' she said.

Pride helps us to stay in denial. It keeps us from admitting that we have not ridden through a particular experience unscathed, or, sometimes, that others have the power to hurt us at all.

As we have seen, what begins as a conscious action can, if it is effective and if it is repeated enough, become automatic. As we shall see in Part Four, it can also become so much a part of us that we simply cannot recognise that we are doing it at all. Furthermore, once we have succeeded in getting painful memories and feelings 'out of sight', we can be extremely reluctant to bring them back. We may have lost track of just what is down there, and be fearful of what will happen if it all comes to the surface.

If we continue in denial, we lie to ourselves, and hold ourselves away from true healing. We need the Holy Spirit in His convicting capacity to bring us out into an acceptance of the truth. If we want Him to, He can always open the eyes of our minds and hearts, so that we can acknowledge past hurts, and their true effect on our development. He can also ensure that only what we can handle at any one time is released into our conscious mind and our feelings. With the Holy Spirit's help we can safely and effectively submit the hurts of the past to the forgiving process.

4. Fear of being orphaned

We all need someone to hold on to, and belong to. We need someone we can trust, look up to, and depend on to guide us. We need someone to whom our lives are of special concern – someone who knows us thoroughly, and daily pursues our best interests.

The people who are primarily given this role are our natural parents. It is impossible to measure how important they are as companions and anchors in our lives. When they let us down, the effect can be devastating.

We each have such a deep and strong desire to have parents who are there for us in these ways that, when they are not, it can be hard to face. Instead of acknowledging what has been missing, we often resort to pretence. We turn a blind eye to their shortcomings, and make believe that they were all that we wanted them to be. Linda, for example, told us: 'I had convinced myself that I'd had a great childhood.'

Once we have created this kind of illusion, we tend to cling on to it for all we are worth. We do this because we think that to face the truth will be to stare into a black hole that will never go away – the abyss of orphanhood. We fear that, in those areas where we acknowledge that our parents were not there for us, we will have to face being parentless for ever.

Understandable though this fear is, for the Christian there is no basis for it, and we must focus on the truth instead.

As we have already seen, God is able to come supernaturally and be a father to us. He is also able to make up retrospectively for the failures of our natural parents to nurture us as He would have wished, and to heal us – **and that starts now**. As we press on with our part in the healing process we can expect, more than ever before, to find Him there for us.

One of the things that I (Richard) had to face as a part of my healing process was that, from the age of eight, my father was not there for me. From the time I started at boarding school, our contact became limited to a few lines of writing a week. Though he seemed interested in the bare bones of my more important achievements in the academic or sporting fields, we could never talk properly about these or the hundred and one other things that concern a small boy every day.

One result of this was that, despite much inspiring teaching on the importance and value of daily prayer, I found it extremely difficult ever to speak to God for more than a few moments here and there. If I had a major spiritual project that I wanted His help with, or some big news to tell Him, I could pray. But after this the little boy inside me would take over. He still thought that God expected him just to get on with the rest of life on his own. Trying to pray about my day-to-day concerns would seem like talking to someone who had lost interest.

Though it has been sad and painful to face all that my father and I did not share, doing so has led not only to a much better relationship with him, but also to my coming to see God for the wonderfully interested and caring Father that He really is.

In many places in the Bible God almost pleads with us to let Him be the ultimate rock in our lives. 'Believe in me!' he says. The Greek word that we translate as 'believe' is *pisteuo*. This means to hold on to, to trust, to depend on. So when God asks us to 'believe' in Him, He is offering to be all that we could ever want in a parent. He promises, through His Son:

> *'I will not leave you orphans – comfortless, desolate, bereaved, forlorn, helpless – I will come [back] to you.'*   (John 14:18)

And the Psalmist confirms what I and many others have experienced, when he states, as a matter of fact:

> *'I have depended upon you since birth;*
> *you have always been my God ...*
> *For if my father and mother should abandon me,*
> *you would welcome and comfort me*
>   [*adopt me as* (your) *child* – Amplified].'*
>   (Psalm 22:10 & 27:10 LB)

We need not fear facing the truth about our past relationships with our parents. Indeed, as we do this, we can look forward with confidence both to seeing those relationships change for the better, and to a new experience of the fatherhood of God.   –

5. Forgiving too quickly

We may see the logic of forgiving; we may know who we
need to forgive and what for; we may have overcome all the
above barriers to forgiving, but still not **feel** ready to do it. In
this case, it would be premature and wrong, and God would
not want us to try.

We deal with this situation in Chapter 14, under 'Emotion
Storing', and in Chapter 16, under 'Step 9'.

PART FOUR

SURRENDERING OUR UN-CHRIST-LIKENESS

Chapter 9

Identifying Our Sin

'For as [a man] *thinks* **in his heart**, so is he.'
(Proverbs 23:7)

'If we claim to be without sin, we deceive ourselves,
and the truth is not in us. If we confess our sins, he is faithful
and just and will forgive us our sins, and purify us from all
unrighteousness [... **everything not in conformity to His will
in purpose, thought, and action** – Amplified].
If we claim we have not sinned, we make him out to be a liar,
and his word has no place in our lives.'
(1 John 1:8–10 NIV)

'When He, the Spirit of Truth ... comes, He will guide you into
all the truth – the whole, full truth ... And when He comes,
He will **convict and convince** the world ... about sin ... '
(John 16:13 & 8)

'**Repent**, for the kingdom of heaven is near.'
(Matthew 4:17 NIV)

When we forgive we take our inner eyes off those people who
have failed us. We free the needy child inside ourselves to
look only to Jesus for what our souls need. We exchange the
insufficient for the All-sufficient.

As we saw in Part One, it is **through relationship** that our
souls receive God's truth-bearing love. How well we relate to

God depends on **how clearly we see Him**. So, once He has our full attention, the first thing He will want to do is to remove those things in our souls that limit our ability to see Him as He is and to relate to Him without hindrance, and so stop us receiving His transforming touch.

Like forgiving, this will also call for action from us.

Whatever is a part of our souls is our property. It is ours to keep or to give away, as we choose. Jesus cannot unilaterally delve inside us and remove those things that inhibit our relationship with Him. We must hand them over ourselves – one by one.

The tool of repentance

To enable us to give away the un-Christ-likeness in our souls, we have been given a second tool to use alongside forgiveness: repentance.

As with forgiveness, our experience is that there are many who do not understand what true, effective repentance is. So, before we go any further, we want to explain this.

What repentance is

Repentance is not simply 'saying sorry' to God.

At its lowest, 'saying sorry' can be an extremely shallow gesture. We can do it simply to get **ourselves** off the hook. It can mean no more than that we are sorry **for ourselves**, and for the mess that our sin has got **us** into – with God or with our fellow men. It can simply be a quick and convenient way to solve the immediate problems (for example disapproval, or, worse still, rejection) that our sin has brought **upon us**.

True repentance involves much more than this. It is a three-stage process. The first is to clearly grasp how a sin affects God, ourselves, and others. The second is to deal with the pain and guilt that this engenders, by giving these up to God to be wiped out by His forgiveness. And the third is to open our souls up to Him, and give Him permission to take away the wrong thinking and behaviour that is rooted there.

The process **may** end in words spoken to God, but it starts with **seeing ourselves for what we are**, and feeling true regret, shame, and sorrow for this, and for its effects all round. It means the full truth about ourselves and our sin, from God's perspective, coming home to our spirits. We need to become progressively more and more 'convicted and convinced' of those inner things that distinguish us from Christ the man.

True repentance is impossible without true conviction. And true conviction is a work of the Holy Spirit.

God's convicting Holy Spirit

God cannot simply wrench our un-Christ-likeness from us. But He can help us to give it away by identifying it for us. Through the Holy Spirit's illuminating work, He can show us all the ways in which, through the soul-building process that we have described, we fall short of the perfection of Christ's own inner make-up.

Once He has done this, we have all the information that we need to consciously and specifically hand over those imperfections to God, and to create the space that He needs to be able to come inside us and change us.

An unwelcome function of the Holy Spirit

We should welcome this help, yet for many of us the prospect of being convicted of sin is the least appealing part of the healing process, if not of our entire Christian lives. If this is so, then we are labouring under misconceptions, and we need to be free of them.

Like everything else that the Holy Spirit does, His work of conviction is a good work. It is designed only to bless and to benefit us. It is the pathway to wholeness.

We have described Christian healing as an exchange – we give away our inner imperfections, and receive Christ-likeness in exchange. There is a direct link between the amount we give away and the extent to which the Holy

Spirit can change us. Not only this, but the surrender of sin into God's forgiveness also brings with it a wonderful sense of relief.

Before we can give anything away, however, we have to identify it and consciously select it for despatch. This is because we have free will, and because, as we have said, everything that is part of our souls is our personal property.

The deeper and wider we can throw the net around our sin, the greater the scope for change within us, and the greater the potential for relief. We should, therefore, welcome with open arms this sin-identifying work of the Holy Spirit.

The truth, however, is that many of us would instinctively rather do almost anything other than be brought face to face with the true extent of our own sin. Why is this?

We believe there are two main reasons. The first is that very often we cannot separate being convicted from being rejected. We think that the two go hand in hand. The conditional human love that has surrounded many of us throughout life has powerfully linked being loved with being good and getting things right, in our minds. It has not shown us a God who loves and accepts us all the time, and wants to help us stay free of sin. Often, when we have admitted wrongdoing, we have been met with disapproval rather than acceptance. Being found out has brought not relief but rejection. So, far from welcoming being confronted with our sin, we greatly fear it.

We are all deeply imperfect, so we get things wrong all the time. Knowing this, and yet wanting at all costs to avoid the feelings of rejection that have come with owning up to our sin in the past, we have learned to play a game. We keep our wrongdoing and failure as far from our conscious minds as possible – often denying it completely. By doing this, we evade that sense of rejection.

This is the first reason that we do not welcome the Holy Spirit's convicting work: we believe that to invite conviction is to invite rejection. The second reason is that we believe that it is also to invite punishment.

For many of us our childhood experience was that to be found guilty, even if we were to say we were sorry, was to be punished rather than forgiven. The world has often sought to beat our sin out of us. It has used 'electric shock treatment' to try to deter us. By doing this it has taught us that, on top of the pain and shame of simply becoming aware of our wrongdoing, conviction from outside will generally earn us an extra dose of physical, emotional, and spiritual pain. It is no wonder that we do not welcome this!

God's approach is not like this at all. His overriding priority is to know us in a close and enriching relationship. Through such a relationship, He wants us to have the very best quality of life available. He rejects not us but our sin, which inhibits that relationship and all that it can bring us. His priority is therefore to push forward a process that lets Him lift our sin out of us – a process that starts with convicting and convincing us of that sin.

In Christ we see a God who bends over backwards to make the removal of our sin and its all round effects as quick, painless, and inexpensive to us as possible.

Every time we are convicted, and see that sin and those effects as He does, this will of course make us feel bad about the way we are, and the things we have done. But, however bad they may be, such feelings are only ever momentary compared to the lasting benefit that lies beyond them. God has put them there simply to motivate us to confess, and to complete the process of repentance as quickly and thoroughly as we can, and to deter us from making the same mistakes again.

Imagine that you often forget to brush your teeth. Decay and toothache result. You know from past experience that your dentist is a master at putting dental problems right quickly and skilfully, and that visiting him is the answer. Even so, you know that the treatment is likely to cause you a few minutes of discomfort. You strongly suspect that your own neglect is the reason that you now need to visit him, and that he is likely, purely to help you to avoid a repeat in the future, to tell you this.

Do you make an appointment to visit him? Or, fearing the brief physical and psychological discomfort that this will involve, do you put up with increasing decay and pain indefinitely?

The choice for most of us will be simple. We will decide that the long-term gain is well worth the short-term pain, and book an appointment as soon as we can.

God, too, is a kind of dentist! Infinitely caring and gentle, His speciality is extracting our sin and replacing it with Christ-likeness. When we sense that we need to see Him, we should not hesitate. And yet we so often do – held up by pride or guilt, but more than anything by a fear that He will treat us in the same way as authority figures have in the past.

The consequence of owning up to them was often not forgiveness and release from a guilty conscience but a sentence. Coming clean about our failures has thus become synonymous in our thinking with rejection and punishment, whereas owning up to God in fact brings immediate relief. In Christ, rather than rejection and punishment, we find acceptance and release.

God is in the business of putting spiritual and emotional decay right, not of hitting us with a big stick! We know this in our heads. We have, for example, read the parable of the Prodigal Son. But the little boy or girl inside us is often not so sure. Past experience tells them something else. Given this, their goal (unsurprisingly) has tended to be to minimise and to bury away their sins as much as they can. They have gratefully laid hold of any device that offered an escape from having to own up and face the consequences of those sins. As we act more and more on the truth that we have a God who is on our side, who brings freedom, and who loves us no matter what, and experience this truth for ourselves, it becomes easier and easier to welcome His convicting Spirit.

Confession – taking responsibility for our sin

As we come to see conviction in a new light, and to realise that the deeper and wider we throw the net around our sin, the greater the release and relief we receive, we can say to God without fear: 'Show me **all my sin**.'

When we do this, one of the first things we may discover is that God's idea of what we are responsible for and ours are somewhat different!

There are direct consequences to **everything** that we think and do. For all of these, we are responsible. The good that emanates from us generates an inner peace. It also sows blessing for us and for others. Likewise, the bad generates guilt and sows harm. Both we ourselves and those we deal with reap all that we sow – both good and bad.

Christ's death on the cross bought us full forgiveness for all of our sins. As we have seen, to apply this forgiveness to any area of our sinful nature, we have to personally surrender the sin concerned. This means recognising it, taking responsibility for it, and repenting of it. We have to say 'Hello' before we can say 'Goodbye'.

It is easy enough to accept this principle for conscious wrong thoughts and actions – things which we were aware we were thinking and saying, and which, at the same time, we knew were wrong. But what about those thoughts and actions that came automatically; those things that came from a deeper place than our conscious minds; those things to which we gave not a second thought at the time; those things that were the result simply of who we are? Does God hold us responsible for these as well?

The crucial test is choice. In all cases where we make a choice to think and act in a particular way, no matter how great the internal or external pressure that may be brought to bear upon us, we are responsible.

It is not difficult to see choice operating in those wrong things that we think or do consciously. But what about those automatic, unconscious thoughts and actions that go on all the time? Can we be said to be choosing to think those thoughts, or to carry out those actions?

The answer is: yes.

Certainly no one else is responsible for what we think and do. This is plain. And yet can we be said to be truly choosing to think and to do what is, by definition, thought or done 'without thinking'?

Again, the answer is: yes.

This is because, as the Bible tells us, all our wrong thoughts and actions ultimately have their source **within us**. It is also because, as we saw in Chapter 2, we ourselves choose how to programme the inner computer that underlies and drives our every wrong thought and action.

From the moment we exist as people in the womb, we are choosing beings. Many of the un-Christ-like things we think and do today will undoubtedly be automatic and unconscious. But (with two exceptions – to which there are also solutions in Christ, and which we discuss later) it is our own choices of the past, building us into the people that we are, that are responsible for the automatic and unconscious things that we think and do today.

We can illustrate how widely choice dictates what we are, and hence what we think and do, in this way:

I (Richard) wear contact lenses. I have done so for many years. The day I first wore them, they were like grit in my eyes. I have now become so used to them that only the improved vision that they give me reminds me that they are there. Something else has changed, too.

Before I started wearing lenses, I automatically blinked when something came near my eyes, let alone got into them. Through necessity, and with practice, I learned to suspend this natural defensive reaction. Keeping my eyes open to insert the lenses each day now comes quite naturally. Strongly motivated by the desire to see clearly again, I overcame my once automatic reaction.

What was natural before was to blink. I did it without thinking. In that sense I would have found it hard, at that time, to have seen my reaction as a choice. I would have said that I 'just blinked'. But now that I know that I can control my blinking, I can no longer argue that I had no choice but to blink.

It is the same with our sin make-up. This is built up by spontaneous reaction at speed to a variety of people and events that bear upon us. Nevertheless, it still has choice at its root. And, since it does, we are responsible for all of it.

If, rather than accepting responsibility for all that we are that is un-Christ-like, we limit our responsibility to our conscious and deliberate wrong thoughts and actions, what we are really saying to God is this: 'Because my make-up has become so different from Christ's, and I am so adept, discreet, and quick at making sinful choices, I should be entitled to disown responsibility for any results of this.'

Thinking this way may help us to hide from the full extent to which we have drifted away from being like Jesus over the years. But it will certainly not help us to give away those things in our souls that block the transforming work of the Holy Spirit. We need instead to understand that accepting responsibility for all our choices, and allowing the Holy Spirit to fully illuminate our sin make-up, will bring approval, forgiveness, and release, rather than rejection, punishment, and pain. If we do, then we open wide the door to deep transformation.

As we saw in Chapter 2, the encyclopaedia of Jesus' soul was different from our own. At its centre was a true picture of God. His spirit and soul always worked together to make the right choices. They chose always to think and to do what was perfectly in tune with God, and right in His eyes. They chose to maintain the God-filled structure of His soul intact and unaltered. For one who had been close to God for as long as He had, such choice was, in a sense, inevitable.

We might be tempted to say that Jesus had no real choice. But this is not true. He was human, just like us. Like us, He had free will. It was simply that any wrong choices on offer made no sense to Him. Perfect reaction to the world around Him was automatic.

To be serious about change is to invite the supernatural, convicting light of the Holy Spirit to show us the difference between what came naturally to Jesus and what comes naturally to us. When we do this we allow God to come and work in us in a deeper way than ever before. At this point true Christ-likeness enters our grasp, and with it the prospect of an unparalleled quality of life and health.

Chapter 10

Sin Conditions

*'Now if I do what I do not desire to do, it is no longer I doing it
– it is not myself that acts – but the sin [principle] which
dwells within me [**fixed and operating in my soul**].'*
(Romans 7:20)

Once we are truly open to His convicting work, the Holy
Spirit finds little difficulty in showing us our deliberate
wrong thoughts or actions. At the time for confession during
a Sunday service, for example, it usually takes only a few
moments for these to come to our minds. This is especially so
if they are recent.

What is much harder for us is recognising those longer-
term patterns of wrong thought and behaviour that are
so much a part of us, so deeply rooted in our souls, and so
habitual that they effectively function on their own – without any conscious decision on our part.

Conscious sin is like peeling paint or cracked roof tiles on a
house. These are superficial defects, and therefore quite easy
to detect and to repair. Unconscious patterns of wrong
thought and behaviour, on the other hand, are more like
advanced woodworm or dry rot in walls and beams. These
forms of decay can be widespread and undermine the very
structure of a house, and yet, because they are often deep-
seated and invisible from the outside, be altogether more
difficult to detect, let alone to put right.

In view of this, we think it helpful to distinguish between conscious wrongdoing and ongoing, and often unconscious, patterns of wrong thought and behaviour. We call the first category sins, and the second sin conditions.

There are a handful of sin conditions that significantly affect nearly all of us. These are continuously at work, undermining the peace, joy and effortlessness of the life that God intends for us. They are also the driving force behind much of our conscious sinning.

It is our experience that, after inaction and unforgiveness, the next biggest obstacle to Christians becoming more like Jesus is our failure to identify and give away sin conditions. Whilst few of us need to be shown an exhaustive list of conscious sins, most of us do need help with recognising and coming to hate our sin conditions. We therefore propose to take a good look at the most common and debilitating of these, making clear how each steals something of the full life that Jesus came to bring us.

'Life in all its fullness'

In order to see sin conditions for the thieves that they are, we need first to have a basic understanding of what Jesus meant by *'life in all its fullness'*.

Living the full life means knowing God as a reality, and experiencing His love at first hand. It means going out from this unshakeable base and enjoying **being what we were made to be**. It also means learning lessons, accomplishing goals, investing in relationships, and carrying out God-given responsibilities. These involve giving out, as well as receiving.

The parable of the Ten Talents reminds us that we are to develop and use the faculties and gifts that God gives us to the full. As we do this, we give Him glory and pleasure, bless others, and make our own unique and essential contribution to the complex and colourful tapestry of life. At the same time we experience maximum fulfilment for ourselves.

So perfect is God's design for life that, if we are living it in the right way, we should find that not only our activities, but also the contented tiredness and the sleep that follows them, are an integral part of life's pleasures.

Jesus offers us life God's way. As we would expect from God's chief ambassador, He too uses the language of activity-without-stress to describe this life. He says:

'My yoke is easy, and my burden is light.'
(Matthew 11:30 NIV)

Christians are not promised fulfilment and victory in life 'on a plate'. We have to sow if we want to reap. We must also expect to meet with both challenge and hardship along the way. What we **are** promised, however, are **resources that are always well equal to any demands God allows life to make upon us**.

Life has its pressures, but their effect on us is relative. How a weightlifter copes with each lift that he makes depends as much on his strength and technique as on the size of the weight that he is lifting. In the same way, how well we cope with life's demands depends on the resources that we have available to us and the use we make of them. What Jesus is saying is that if we are living life **His way** – the right way – then, whatever our circumstances, we will find life, at bottom, inwardly comfortable and invigorating, rather than stressful and draining.

An 'easy yoke' and a 'light burden' come from having inner resources that are always well equal to the demands that God places upon us.

This is how things should be. Yet many of us in fact find living life more of an effort than we should. We find ourselves constantly overburdened and stretched – occasionally beyond breaking-point. As a result we find varying degrees of stress and fatigue our constant companions. Where these persist, feelings of discouragement, and sometimes even depression, can set in as well.

If life is a burden, then our inner resources are being overtaxed. Yet God Himself never loads us up with more than we can handle. If our resources are not well equal to the life we are living – either the level of those resources is lower than it should be, or we are draining ourselves in ways that God never intended that we should.

There are of course those times when we know that we are taking on too much. But there are others when we feel over-burdened for no apparent reason – times when our lives should be comparatively plain sailing, yet we feel as if we are walking in glue!

At the root of such experiences are sin conditions.

Sin conditions – Satan's life-stealers

All sin conditions are the result of wrong perspectives on life that we have built into our souls. They burden not only our souls, but our spirits and bodies as well.

Working together, they do this in two ways:

1.   They choke us off from the full amount of inner resource that God intends each of us to have available to us – the same level of resource that was available to Christ the man.
2.   They lock us into overactivity, which unnecessarily drains us.

Imagine you need to make an urgent and speedy car journey across a desert. You measure the distance in miles, and calculate that provided you completely fill your tank with petrol, and are the only one in the car, you will comfortably reach your destination.

Imagine that, instead of doing this, you not only half fill your tank, but then give a lift to a group of hitchhikers, each with a large rucksack.

An irrational thing to do? Yes, of course. But this is exactly how we approach our own journeys through life, for as long as we allow sin conditions to reign within us. They mean that we are **both under-resourced and overtaxed at the same time** – that we are constantly doing too much, with too little inner energy. They supplant Christ's 'easy yoke' and 'light burden' with something perpetually onerous. Occasionally, they can even cause us to break down totally.

Each of the sin conditions that we shall describe has its own unique ingredients. But they all operate in this dual way to erode the full life that God intends each of us to enjoy, and to take away the radiance that is our birthright as Christians.

The source of sin conditions

Most sin conditions have their roots at deep levels of our souls. They are so much a part of us that we often cannot see them for what they are.

We have described our souls as self-compiled, inner encyclopaediae, which advise our spirits on their path through life. God intends their 'pages' to be filled up with truth. But we receive and build **misinformation** into them. It is this misinformation that is the driving force behind sin conditions.

Most common sin conditions

During our time in this ministry, we have found that there are six sin conditions that most commonly affect people. These are:

- False Judging
- Love Earning
- Overload Bearing
- Emotion Storing
- Controlling
- Love Substituting

Every one acts as a firm 'No Entry' sign to the Holy Spirit. Yet, widespread though they are, they often go completely undetected among Christians. The next four chapters will therefore describe each in some detail.

Chapter 11

False Judging

*'Blessed are the **pure in heart**, for they shall **see** God!'*
(Matthew 5:8)

*'The spiritual man **makes judgments** about all things...'*
(1 Corinthians 2:15 NIV)

Making judgments – a God-given ability

God has given us all the ability to make judgments about people. To use this gift correctly is **to truly and accurately gauge** what people are like, and where they are at. If love is an accurate measure and supply of a person's needs, then making judgments is vital to being able to love others, and ourselves, properly.

This has nothing to do with assessing people's lives with a view to rewarding them or passing final sentence on them. That is God's business, not ours.

The ability to make judgments is not only vital to the proper giving of love. It also enables us, in this fallen world, to protect ourselves and those under our care. It tells us, for example, who to trust and who to be guarded with. Being able to make judgments is thus crucial to the quality of our relationships, and to living the full life.

False Judging

To judge falsely is to draw conclusions about people that are wrong.

We are all guilty of False Judging. It is the most serious and far-reaching sin condition of all, and **it lies behind all the others.**

We can falsely judge anyone. But False Judging is seen at its most damaging in our relationship with God. It results in our carrying a defective picture of Him around inside us. This prevents us seeing Him as He really is, and knowing what He is really like, which, in turn, cripples our relationship with Him, and limits our ability to receive from Him.

The reason for this, as we began to see in Part One, is that the way we see someone dictates how we relate to them. If we like what we see, we are drawn to them, and we open ourselves to them. The more of their characteristics we like, the closer we are drawn to them, and the more we open ourselves to them. If, on the other hand, we do not like what we see, we retreat and put up defensive barriers. The less we like about them, the more we do this.

This is also true of our relationship with God. In every way in which we decide that He is less wonderful than He really is, we become that much more distant from Him and closed to Him. The effect is that we are starved of Him.

We are, quite literally, made for God. He made us with the capacity to be receptive to Him, in a way that we cannot be to anyone else. This does not mean that we are therefore compelled to be in full and perfect communion with Him. We are not robots. But what it does mean is that the more we see Him as He really is, the more deeply we want Him.

To see God **in every way as He really is** is to love and to want Him **with our whole being.** This leads automatically to the dismantling of defensive barriers, which, in turn, enables us to absorb all that He is and all that He has to give us by His Spirit. Once we get to this position we **will** receive fully, because, as the Bible tells us, He longs to give us good things (Psalm 84:11; Matthew 7:7–11).

When we make wrong judgments about our fellow human beings, we diminish our fellowship with them. When we judge God falsely we cut ourselves off from so much more. He is perfect. He is love. He is all-powerful. He is the ultimate and only provider of every good thing that we could ever need to resource and sustain us – including safe supernatural healing. Nothing is more resource-depriving than falsely judging God.

Why we judge falsely

All judging involves analysing information. For example, we may observe two men some distance away. Seeing one gesture angrily at the other, we may make a snap decision that he is unpleasant and to be avoided. We may see the other as a victim, and feel inclined to go to his defence.

However, when we judge, we do not look only at what is physically in front of us. We also automatically draw on information from past experiences that is stored in our souls. This crucially affects the way we see people.

For example, if in our families we had only ever experienced righteous anger, we might see our two men quite differently. We might instinctively side with the angry man, and cast the 'victim' in the role of villain.

By giving us souls, God has made it possible for us to learn by experience, and to draw on stored information about people in the past to assess people in the present. Relying on this stored information, we continuously judge people and situations, and steer our preferred path through life. We avoid what does not appeal to us and gravitate towards what does. Our ability to store information as we go along means that we have the potential to make progressively better and better judgments about people.

We judge God in the same soul-informed way. Whilst some of the information about Him in our souls is drawn from our own direct experience of Him as Christians, the rest comes to us 'indirectly' through His designated human agents – most importantly our parents.

As we have seen, God's design for our development is such that how these agents are and how they interact with us always implants a picture of God inside us. Of course He wants that picture to be one that accurately reflects what He is really like. But the effect of their faults is to implant deep within us information about what He is like that is partially (and often seriously) false. Until this is specifically removed and replaced with truth about God, we continue, from our souls, to lay their likeness, and their imperfect view of Him, onto Him. **We see Him as being partly like them, and partly as they see Him.**

Because we absorb this indirect information about God into our souls from the very beginning of our lives, it has an overriding influence on our judgments. Though we may think that the information that we hold in our conscious minds makes up our picture of Him, it is actually what is held at deeper levels that decides this. Through the judging process, our experience of people in the past governs how in truth we see and relate to God.

In this situation, our judging mechanism is alive and functioning. But we are being misled by false information that is still stored deep in our souls. Seeing God as being as He is portrayed by our fallible key nurturers means that, in our deepest places, we are as closed to Him as we are to them. Defences and barriers that we put up against their short-comings have the effect of keeping Him out as well. We also see His superhuman aspects as they did.

We are all guilty of False Judging, because we have all been fed misinformation. This means that whatever we may think in our conscious minds, at the level that really matters our relationship with God will always be a mirror image of our relationships with our key nurturers, and of their relationships with God.

We looked at some of the hidden dynamics of our human relationships in Chapter 3. Figure 29 may help to illustrate how False Judging incorporates these into our relationship with God.

Figure 29

The experience of Tom, now a fully ordained Church of England clergyman, provides a good example of this.

Tom was part way through his two year ordination course at theological college when he came for counsel. The career he had chosen was evidence of his commitment. His desire was to know God better, and to serve Him wholeheartedly in what he believed was a calling to the overseas mission field. At the same time he was aware of both an underlying reluctance to get too close to God, and continuing doubts about whether he had what it took to do this kind of work. These two negative undercurrents had been like a black cloud, first over a trip Tom had made to China for practical training on the mission field, and then over his time at theological college. He found the inner conflict that they caused him a perpetual drain.

During our time with Tom it emerged that his father, rather than pinpointing and affirming his God-given person-ality and gifting, and then encouraging him down the path that Tom himself would have chosen, had imposed his own aspirations on him. It was here that the roots of the conflict inside Tom lay. He later wrote:

'I would like to register my appreciation for the ministry I received from you over the last two weeks. I believe that the Holy Spirit revealed certain things to me that were highly significant.

For too long I have served the Lord out of a sense of duty rather than love. I believed that God was like my earthly father, and was trying to manipulate me and force His own agenda on my life. Thus, although I strove to obey Him, in my heart I felt resentful.

Because of a false vision of God, at times I have been wary to spend time in prayer getting to know God intimately – just in case He spoke and told me to do something I didn't want to do. I no longer feel that is the case. I know that God does not want to force me to do anything. Yes, He knows what is best for me. But I have my free will, and can serve Him not out of duty but love.'

The false judgments, based on his earthly father, that Tom had made against God were distorting his view of God, and making Him an unattractive and risky God to serve. They were also keeping Him at arm's length, and cutting Tom off from the resource of His affirming and healing love.

Surrendering these false judgments to God opened the way for him to see God as the sensitive Father that He really is. It also removed the barriers that until then had kept His love from reaching the parts of Tom that had been deprived. With these barriers out of the way, that love could begin its affirming and healing work – both directly and through human agents. He went on:

'I had also felt ill-equipped and unsure I knew exactly what God was calling me to do. This led to a feeling of restlessness and dissatisfaction. Thankfully this has begun to change. Deep down I can now acknowledge how much I have grown spiritually. I have been encouraged that many people seem to recognise gifts God has given me, and feel increasingly affirmed in my call to this ministry. In fact I now thank God that He led me to China and has given me this call to study at college.'

Tom's story underlines how False Judging, founded on our parents' shortcomings, can cut us off from the resource of God's affirming and guiding love. It also shows how it can detract from our relating to God as a source of refreshment and joy, making this a drain instead. As long as the wrong information about God on which Tom's judgments were based remained stored in his soul, this state of affairs persisted. But once the memory banks that held this information were broken into, and it had been surrendered, there was room for God to bring in a new, true picture of Himself.

This is what happened to Susan, who we met in Chapter 3. As we took her through the 'Double Agenda', the Holy Spirit showed her how her father's remoteness and his constant rebuffs had affected her view of God. Seeing this was the first step to surrendering the misinformation in her soul to the cleansing work of the Holy Spirit, and to receiving a new picture of God. Where once she had viewed Him as distant and out of touch with her, she now came to see Him as He really is.

As well as being remote, Susan's father, who was from a strict religious background, expected high standards of behaviour from her. Because of this she believed not only that God's love was in short supply, but also that she had constantly to perform very well to get even the little that was going.

Just as it had in my (Richard's) case, the information in Susan's soul had led to her becoming deeply run down and depressed. She was heading for the same kind of emotional and physical standstill that I had reached. At the same time she continued to try to carry out all the responsibilities of a conscientious wife of a pressurised company chief executive, and of a mother of three young children.

Here is her moving and honest description of the beginnings of the arrival in her soul of a new, true picture of God:

'It seems so hard to write this letter. It's very difficult to gather my thoughts together to make sentences even. I feel devoid of all emotion except depression. I can't be bothered to do very much around the house. My appetite has completely gone, and I have no desire to see or speak to anyone. Doing anything at all is an immense effort.

Putting myself in a position where God can speak to me is easier said than done. The feeling of depression, and the tiredness that comes with it, is a huge barrier to opening the Bible on my own. To pray a "Dear Lord Jesus" prayer requires too great a concentration of thought. Reading anything other than a tabloid newspaper is also difficult.

Although the struggles of day-to-day living are painfully obvious, through it all I still feel the hand of God on me. Something within my heart has witnessed to the fact that, in the short term, I can be anything in the presence of God, and it will be okay. His love for me is big enough to handle it. I don't believe for one second that I will feel this depressed all my life, but for now I believe it's okay to be like this in the presence of God. Sometimes I pray that He will lift it – sometimes I don't. But either way I'm aware of Him working something out in my life.

I feel I have built on the sand, and that God has turned His spotlight on my building, and it's mostly crumpled. I feel as though my mind has been blown. I'm starting again in my knowledge of both God and me. And this is where I am:

1. That I can be truly me, express my emotions and words in the presence of God, and His love and attitude towards me will be exactly the same.

2. Because faithfulness is part of His character He is committed to changing me into His likeness, with ever increasing glory. All I need is to have an open, sincere heart towards Him.

3. His desire is for me to receive every blessing He has for me.

4. I know His knowledge of me is so great and so personal that He knows the groans of my heart; that the times I sit in His presence unable to say anything, He knows the things I am unable to put into words.'

This was just the beginning. As this new, true picture of God settled in Susan's soul, the depression lifted, and she was able to write to us again and to say:

'Looking back over the last few months, I see the hand of God so clearly moving over my life. It fills me with joy **knowing Him, and being loved by Him!**'

During her healing process the Holy Spirit entirely changed the landscape of Susan's soul. He replaced the old messages about God and about men with new ones. He did this by bringing home to her deepest places that He is a sensitive and gentle Father, who longs to know us and to communicate His heart to us. He showed her that not all men were necessarily like her natural father. In doing this He enabled her to come out from behind her defences, and to begin to enjoy a much closer relationship with her husband.

'We've talked more in the last four weeks than in the last four years!' she was soon telling us.

'Seeing' as Jesus did

We saw in Chapter 2 that an accurate picture of God was the central and dominant feature in Jesus' soul. Everything that

He thought and did during His earthly life was anchored in the fact of God's existence, of His perfect nature and love, of His infinite power, and of His sovereign control in all areas.

As well as dominating His entire outlook on life, this soul-knowledge of God enabled Jesus to experience unhindered unity and communication with Him. He was open and receptive to every beat of God's heart of pure love. In His Sermon on the Mount, Jesus said, *'Blessed are the **pure in heart**, for they shall **see God**.'* Until our souls give up false information about God, deep down we will never be able to see Him as He really is, or to receive all that He has to offer us. Instead we will be at war with Him, distance ourselves from Him, and shut Him out. Tom and Susan's experiences show both how disabling such information can be, and just how radically our own relationships with God can move forward when it is replaced with truth.

We have especially emphasised the consequences of False Judging when it relates to God. This is because everything else flows from the quality of our relationship with Him. However, our relationships with other people are a significant ingredient of the full life too. Just as we can falsely judge God on the basis of our human relationships, so also we can falsely judge one human being on the basis of our relationship with another – with important consequences.

Much of the blessing that God plans for our lives is designed to come to us through our fellow men and women. So the limitations that False Judging puts on our ability to assess others accurately, to meet them where they are, and to be open to receive from them too, do matter. The difference is that the strengthening of our relationship with God, and the healing that this releases into us, is the key to enhancing our relationships with our fellow human beings.

Jesus was nobody's doormat. He chose to remain in open and unprotected heart-communication with every person that He met, no matter how insensitive or cruel they might be to Him. He chose to bear the full consequences of this. It was His perfect and unfettered relationship with the Father, continuously resourcing Him and healing any wounding, that made this possible.

As we surrender our false judgments about God to Him, He gains new access to us. By His Spirit He strengthens us, heals us, and brings in truth that enables us to see others as He does – as they really are, and not as we have falsely judged them to be. He is also better able to resource us with His empowering love. This means that we, like Jesus, can go on loving others accurately from our hearts, and being truly open to them. Whereas God and other people have until now been blurred by our False Judging, we can look forward to conducting our relationships with both through increasingly clear spectacles.

Chapter 12

Love Earning

*'Yes, I have loved you with **an everlasting love**.'*
(Jeremiah 31:3)

*'God **is love**...'*
(1 John 4:16)

Love Earning is doing something with the **underlying purpose** of having others like and accept us. We do this to ensure that they continue to give us spiritually, emotionally, and physically what we want from them. It is 'buying' love by trying to please, and can greatly detract from both the quality of our relationships with God and other people, and our effectiveness for Christ.

Love Earning means constantly tailoring our thoughts and actions to meet what we see as others' expectations of us, for the sake of gaining their approval. This can seriously hold us back from expressing our true feelings, and therefore having our own true needs met. Often, given the imperfections of every human being that we may seek to please, it can prevent us from giving expression to Christ within us, and doing what is right.

Love Earning is driven by fear – fear of causing love sources to withdraw their 'love'. Because of our absolute, paramount need to feel loved, for as long as this fear of losing love remains, we can never really be ourselves.

As Christians, we have by definition begun to get to know a God who exudes a love that neither needs to be, nor can be, earned. Yet many of us continue to be ruled by this fear and persist in trying to earn love – from Him and from other people. Why?

The root of Love Earning

At the root of all Love Earning are false judgments in the soul about what real love is like. These lead us to what is perhaps the single most debilitating conclusion of all time: that **there is no such thing as completely unconditional love, but that all love makes at least some demands on us**.

The misinformation in our souls that leads us to this conclusion consists of past examples of love sources having to be pleased, and withdrawing their love where they were not. From this we conclude that being fully loved always depends, at least to some extent, on thinking and doing the 'right' thing in the eyes of love sources.

Once again it is our key nurturers who feed us this misinformation. None are able to love us with a love that is always and absolutely uninfluenced by our behaviour. None show us a perpetually smiling heart. This means that deep down we simply have no concept of the perfect, constant, inexhaustible, and unfluctuating love that God offers. Instead we believe that God's love is 'love' as our parents and other key nurturers demonstrate it: a resource that is kept flowing by our being what they want us to be.

Some of us shape our whole lives around the belief that, even with God, how much love we get depends on how we behave. We read in the Bible that God's love is always freely available. We know in our heads that this must be true. But, deeper down, the child who experienced only conditional love, believes something quite different, and forces us to earn love.

A way of life

Love Earning shows through in many of the real-life stories that we have already told. My own (Richard's) story shows the extremes to which it can lead. But many who already know Jesus, whilst they would have little difficulty in accepting the statement that God's love for them is unconditional, would, at the same time, admit that they were very far from being free to be completely themselves in all situations.

When we become Christians, we enter a direct relationship with an unconditionally loving God. This should prove the perfect antidote to Love Earning. But what happens in practice is often the reverse. Having found a better quality of love within the Body of Christ than we ever experienced from the world, and still believing that no love is truly free, we work even harder to keep this new love coming! We become increasingly clear about what **God** wants of us, but we try to do this not out of gratitude for a love that we know we cannot lose, but in an effort to ensure that this love never dries up.

Although love-earners try to please even God for love, pleasing people is their highest priority. Three things come together to cause this. First, the little boy or girl inside each of us had an absolute, insatiable need to be loved. Second, he or she very often knew nothing but love sources made of flesh and blood. And third, he or she experienced only fluctuating 'love'.

Before we are 'born again' into an ability to grasp spiritual realities, we know only relationships with other human beings. This programmes our dictatorial souls to pursue love sources that are detected and experienced through the physical senses of sight, touch, hearing, and smell, rather than towards God, who is spirit, and who is detected and experienced through spiritual and not physical antennae. In short, the prevailing inner belief, held as a result of past experience, goes like this: 'We must have love. God may be there somewhere in the background, but the love that matters comes from physical people. Their "love" demands performance. So we **must** please **people**.' Trying to gain and hold on to the 'love' (or more accurately the approval) of other human beings is thus, by force of habit, our highest priority.

Love Earning enables Satan, from time to time, to quite literally give us hell on Earth. We are never able, inwardly, to rely one hundred per cent on love to be there for us come what may. Satan can pick on any of those categories of thoughts and activities that meant disapproval and rejection (real or perceived) from our key nurturers, and tell us that those same thoughts and activities mean disapproval and rejection from God and others today.

An inadequate picture of love, as God understands and offers it, causes us to be susceptible to trying to earn it. But love is a short word describing something that contains many ingredients. If we are to see clearly how we have misunderstood God's love, and how much we are affected by Love Earning, we need to know what real love is. In Chapter 7 we described God's main goals for our upbring-ings, and how parents and others were to achieve these. But what does it mean to say that God is love, and loves us?

It means all of the following:

- that He has an unshakeable, benevolent mind-set towards us, accompanied by feelings;

- that this forces Him to act caringly and constructively at all times towards the Creation, and towards people in particular, in all sorts of ways;

- that He always has our best interests at heart;

- that He is eternally inclined to like, cherish, value, nurture, affirm, instruct, guide, and protect us, and to provide for all our right needs;

- that He has the resources always to back up these inclinations with appropriate practical action, and to go on doing this forever.

Finally it means that He is primarily concerned to develop us and to free us to be ourselves – the people that He made us to be.

God exists. He always has. He always will. And He **is** one hundred per cent pure love (1 John 4:16). Love emanates consistently and perpetually from Him. He has both the personal qualities and the power to deliver every aspect of **perfect love** to each of us. This means that love of this quality is **always available to us from a love source that is unchanging in spite of anything we think or do.**

As we saw in Chapter 7, God chooses to convey aspects of His love to us through human channels. All are intended only as passing and partial sources of the love that He wants each of us to receive. He stands constantly behind them all, with the perfect power and wisdom that enables Him to deliver it wholly effectively and appropriately at all times. Human channels may be the cause of temporary failures of that love to reach us. But, provided our hearts are open and our spiritual receivers attuned to Him, He can override such failures, and ensure that ultimately we receive it anyway.

It is a failure to understand these eternal and unconditional aspects of real love that gives Love Earning its other key characteristic: **a constant need to get things right.** This is reinforced by the tendency of nurturers to place too much emphasis on one of the two main strands of God's brief for bringing up children, at the expense of the other. Let us explain.

Ephesians 6:4 points to these two strands. Parents and others, it says, should rear children *'[tenderly] in the training and discipline and the counsel and admonishment of the Lord'*. The strands are: acceptance and direction. The one is intended to hold us firmly, and to show us that love is always there. From this basis of secure acceptance, the other is intended take us forward.

Acceptance means parents and others showing understanding, empathy, and approval, and meeting legitimate spiritual, emotional, and physical needs. It also means their showing a child that their own world is crucially improved by that unique child's existence – in other words, that they matter. It is supposed to be given continuously alongside instruction, to kill any suggestion that the child's success or failure in doing what is asked of it has anything to do with its being loved.

Love must instruct. It must sometimes say, 'Do this!' or 'Don't do that!' But it must at all times hug and hold. This demands an emotional giving and effort that many nurturers are either unwilling or unable to find from within themselves. Instead their parenting becomes an exercise in directive force-feeding. Instruction is given as much as anything to suit the convenience of the nurturer's own agenda (for their lives as well as the child's), and is a tool of control and coercion, rather than of genuine enabling for the child.

Many parents allocate their children only a limited amount of space on the map of their own lives. Controlling instruction is their tool for confining them within this space. Children are quick to work out what their parents expect and how to avert their displeasure. This, combined with a total or partial failure of parents to convey the acceptance strand of the 'Double Agenda', forces children to see obtaining a sense of being accepted as being inextricably bound up with getting things right in their parents' eyes.

There is a further twist. 'Right' does not necessarily mean right as God sees it, but rather as selfish, flawed, and unregenerate nurturers see it. This includes their concept of success. The result is that **Christian love-earners can spend much of their time and energy trying to earn a love that is free, by trying to comply with a set of rules and standards that are not God's!**

Our parents should never have rejected us, even if we were doing wrong by God. But they have often done so when the only system we were bucking was their own. The result is that we have learned to comply with their often very personalised sets of 'rules', in order to buy as much approval as we can. Our inner comfort and a sense that we are loved has become powerfully tied to **getting things right** according to their often highly subjective and individual code.

Worse still, this game is not always black and white, or predictable. It can be fraught with fear and uncertainty.

On the one hand we have an innate ability to accept God's perspective on life – to recognise right from wrong, truth from lies, the just from the unfair, and the sensible from the bizarre. The code under which God **intended** us to be brought up contains logical and mutually consistent pillars. It will always make sense to us, even if, at times, in our rebellion, we are drawn to flouting it. If this alone were the code under which we were brought up, we would know at all times that love was there for us. We would also know with certainty what thinking and behaviour would bring us blessing, and what would not.

By contrast, many of the rules that prevail in our homes and schools are haphazard and illogical. They are made up 'as they go along' by the damaged and imperfect people that surround us. These people, with all their imperfections, **are** the rules.

If we were able to understand our parents as God does, we might be able to make more sense of the way they relate to us. We might not only know with certainty what to expect from them in different situations, but also why they react as they do. As it is, we have only a few surface clues to work from. So getting things right is often a hit-and-miss affair, with the need to continuously read the signals coming from them.

Being the self-centred creatures that we are, we tend as children to relate all negative expressions from our key nurturers to ourselves. For example, a naturally tense father comes home from a long day's work. He is drained and disgruntled. His superiors have misunderstood and criticised him. His secretary has had her mind on other things, and made mistakes all day. Though he has no complaint against his seven-year-old son, and does his best to reciprocate his affectionate 'welcome home', he needs space and to offload to his wife. He quickly sends his son off to amuse himself. 'Not just now,' is his response to the little boy's wanting to show him the model railway he has built. However, later in the evening, rested and unwound, he seeks him out and plays with him until bedtime.

Lacking the full picture, the little boy will, unless he is specifically told otherwise, assume that his father's mood and behaviour when he comes home has something to do with him. If the scenario repeats itself, as it most likely will, he will try to earn the love he needs by always making himself scarce when his father first comes home. This seems to be what his father wants, because it is not long before he is being nice to him again. And, though there is none, he makes a connection between doing what his father seems to want and the love that eventually comes his way.

Each and every one of us is created with a permanent need to be loved. In order to be genuinely and completely happy, we need to feel that we are known and understood, valued and liked, and that all our legitimate spiritual, emotional, and physical needs matter to someone and will be met.

Nothing can match a love that does this. Nothing can replace it. By contrast, nothing can match the deprivation or the discomfort of the feelings of rejection that flow from not receiving this kind of love. We simply must have it. So, if it comes at the price of having to think and act in certain prescribed ways, we quickly get into the habit of stumping up that price. The consequences of not doing so are simply too painful to contemplate.

Our need to be loved is not, however, just a matter of comfort. It goes to the very root of our ability to experience the life God intends for us. To enable us to exist, our bodies, which contain our spirits and our souls, must be supplied with the physical resources of oxygen, warmth, water, and food. However, if, beyond merely existing, we are to experience life in any degree of fullness, we need additional resources. We are not just physical machines. We are spiritual and emotional creatures as well. We have spiritual and emotional needs. These, too, crave their own special kind of resources.

God has provided the means by which we can receive the full range of the resources that we need, first to nurture us to maturity, and then to continue to sustain us spiritually and emotionally, until we die. Love, as He sees it, is supplying us with all of these resources.

A performance car is designed to run at its best on pure, high-octane petrol. Without this it may either run less well –

for example, if petrol of a lower strength is used, or it may break down completely – for example, if sand or water are mixed with the petrol. In the same way, a person is designed to run on pure love.

If we are loved as God intends throughout our journey to adulthood, we will experience a love that is strong, accurate, and all-sufficient to meet our God-given needs. We will not only have all the resources that we need to grow up to full maturity, but we will also be secure in the knowledge that God accepts and cherishes us just as we are, and will provide all we need to go on enjoying the full life. We will know that the flow of the resources that we need cannot be diminished in any way by what we do, and that it will never end. We will know, in the fullest sense, what it is to be unconditionally loved.

In God's design, love operates like a food. To have its effect, it has to be continuously swallowed, digested, and absorbed throughout our formative and later years. In order to ensure that we absorb and benefit from this resource as fully as possible, God has created each of us with an all-consuming desire for it. Just as a starving man craves a good square meal, from the moment we are first formed as people we crave this food for life called love.

Spiritually and emotionally, we are, quite literally, made for it. In this sense, receiving the benefits of this resource should come so naturally to us all as to be an effortless exercise. With our own needs for love met to overflowing, we should then be able to enjoy the full life. Furthermore, resourced to become agents of God's love to others, we should all be able to take our place as channels, with God, of an all-sufficient flow of this resource down the generations.

This is how God plans His love to work in the lives of humanity. Love that has a permanent smile in its heart and on its face is interminably available from Him. It is free and without limit. Trying to earn it is thus a nonsense.

In Love Earning we see a condition that is as widespread as it is undetected. Most of us are hugely bound by it and yet only minimally aware that we are. (We defined Love Earning as thinking or acting with the **underlying purpose** of earning 'love'. We did not say **conscious purpose**, because most of our Love Earning comes from a place much deeper than our conscious mind.) It is so automatic that we need the Holy Spirit to show us the full extent of it.

It is partly because Love Earning has been a part of us for so long that we do not see the extent to which it grips us. But there is another reason. This is that we have become masters at not provoking rejection.

So deep and strong is our need to feel loved, and our belief that love does not come free, that we become experts at being what we think 'love' sources want us to be. We are inwardly programmed to change course at the slightest hint of disapproval – long before we provoke full-blown rejection. This means that we rarely get the chance to actually experience its full force, and so to be reminded how painful it would be to us. We thus lose sight of just how much we are controlled by the desire to avoid it.

For this reason, we often only start to realise just what love-earners we are when we try to obey God against the tide of the world around us. It is when we become willing to take risks and to provoke disapproval that we realise just how much we fear being rejected!

Given how crucial it is to us to feel loved, and yet how conditional human love almost always is, it is not difficult to understand why we become such experts at being and doing whatever pleases 'love' sources. What can take longer to see is how much we learn to value, develop, and put on display those things about ourselves that attract their approval. Our sense of self-worth becomes so inextricably bound up with these, and they are so much our priority that, to a far greater extent than most of us ever truly appreciate, **we *are* those things that we have been, and those things that we have done, that have pleased others**. In contrast, those parts of us that have not positively attracted the approval of our 'love' sources, though they never completely die, lie neglected, or even rejected entirely, within us.

Under-resourced and overtaxed

As love-earning Christians we are under-resourced because, concentrating inwardly on the business of earning love, we have simply failed to focus our vision on the unconditional love that is available to us from God, and to receive it. We are overtaxed because from deep down we are continually expending ourselves assessing what we need to do to please 'love' sources, and then trying to do it. We are like people on a hot summer's day, who, wanting to get warm, need only to go outside and bask in the sun, but instead choose to stay inside and ride our exercise bicycles.

The road to freedom

God's love is unconditional and unearnable. Nothing that we can think or do will diminish or increase the supply of it. At the root of all Love Earning are false judgments that deny this truth, lock us into working for love, and close us off from receiving the real thing. The antidote to Love Earning is to actually experience God's love through our relationship with Him. It is ever greater inner exposure to God, and ever deeper absorption of the unconditional love that He radiates. Only this can bring home the message to the little boy or girl inside us that, in Christ, we are unerringly and unshakeably cherished and accepted, regardless of whether we are good or bad, right or wrong.

The key to opening the doors to our souls, and to experiencing God in this way, is identifying our false judgments about His nature and the quality of His love, and handing them over for His forgiveness.

Love Earning involves a culture of self-suppression. It is trying to be something that we are not in order to secure something that will never satisfy us. It is right to want to please God. But this starts with self-surrender. By trying to suppress or control anything we would otherwise think or do out of a fear of being disapproved of, we are not pleasing Him but guilty of trying to earn His love. Rather than suppressing 'wrong' thoughts or actions, we need to surrender those false judgments that force us to earn love, and so open the doors to an increasing experience of the real thing.

Few of us will become free from Love Earning overnight. Most of us will need to wean ourselves progressively from conditional, human love sources. Jesus said,

> *'If you **hold** to my teaching, you are really my disciples. Then you will know the truth and the truth will set you free.'*
> (John 8:31–32 NIV)

If we persist with seeking out the false judgments that underlie this condition, God will, in the end, set us truly free of all Love Earning tendencies. Paul envisaged our becoming *'wholly filled and flooded with God Himself'* in our *'innermost being'*. If we set our face toward this goal, we will find that the truth that He loves us without condition, with a love that can supply our every need, will eventually come to rule our soul.

The prize is great. It is deeper intimacy with God, as judgments and the barriers that they form against Him are removed. It is inner security and self-confidence, as we cease to measure ourselves, and how valuable we are, by how well we once performed and continue to perform in peoples' eyes, and against their scales of value. It is freedom to be ourselves, as the reactions of others pale into insignificance against God's cast-iron acceptance. It is greater effectiveness in the world, as we are freed to think and do what is right, rather than what is convenient or popular.

As all these things happen we become God-pleasers in a new way. We please Him, not **out of fear and to earn love**, but **out of joy and gratitude for love received**. We please God by absorbing more of Him, and so becoming more like Him ... **by being ourselves and being pleasing**, not by being something else just in order to please.

Chapter 13

Overload Bearing

'Come to me, all you who are weary and burdened, and I will give you rest. Take my yoke upon you and learn from me, for I am gentle and humble in heart, and you will find rest for your souls. For my yoke is easy and my burden is light.'
(Matthew 11:28–30 NIV)

God's plan is that our lives should be a pleasure. He does not want stress or strain to have any place in us. But experiencing Jesus' easy yoke and light burden means sticking to one golden rule: we must take on only what He calls us to, and no more.

Overload Bearing breaks this rule. It is an addiction to shouldering responsibility that in God's eyes belongs to others.

Just as they were with Love Earning, false judgments are also at the root of Overload Bearing. Once again these are based on misinformation in the soul, and once again, this misinformation has its source in our key nurturers. It consists of examples of their either struggling or failing entirely to fulfil their responsibilities. From this we conclude that, in a variety of ways, neither God nor other people are fully up to carrying out crucial responsibilities on their own, but need our help to do this.

Starting with the family, a reliable and functioning society is made up of an ordered interweaving of God and people, each using their particular attributes and gifts to fulfil their own separate responsibilities. It is essential to its proper working that all play their part. Thus life as God designed it is held together in a complex pyramid, with God Himself at the top. If we are to comfortably confine ourselves to our own responsibilities in life, we need to be able to depend on others to fulfil theirs. If they do not, we can come under pressure to step in and take them on ourselves.

In Chapter 7 we saw that God delegates specific tasks in the process of bringing us to maturity to our parents and to significant others. His main goal is that they should send each of us out into life with a deep knowledge both of what He is like, and of what it means to be loved unconditionally by Him.

Though we did not actually draw this out, this includes giving us a sense of security. By what they are, what they believe, and what they do, God's agents of truth-bearing love are meant to show us that God exists, that He is perfectly in tune with all our needs as individuals, that He is **all**-mighty, that He cares about us all, and that He can fulfil His responsibility for meeting all our needs.

Through His brief to key nurturers, God has made provision for each of us to be filled with this knowledge and the sense of security that it brings. So long as they play their part, we can all grow up living within what we call God's 'Security Arch'.

For much of the time that we have been Christians, we have attended traditional Church of England fellowships. So, like many other western Christians, we are used to worshipping within ancient buildings that have stood for centuries. The stones that make them up are often several feet thick. They look as if even an earthquake would not shake them!

Buildings like this, with their solid floors, walls, and roofs, provide an apt illustration of the structure that God intends should surround each of us in our early years, to provide us with spiritual, emotional, and indeed physical security. This is why we refer to this structure as God's 'Security Arch'.

We can depict life within this Arch using Figure 30.

God's security arch
(our parents)

Figure 30

A stone arch of the kind that we have in mind gives us a solid floor under our feet, strong walls around us, and a reliable roof over our heads. In God's spiritual, emotional, and physical 'Security Arch' there is a floor that bears the full weight of all that we are. This allows us to be ourselves, without having to hold back. There are walls that surround us, like arms. These hold us, and give us safe boundaries. Finally, there is a roof over our heads. This protects us.

At this point the stone arch in our analogy needs some imaginative embellishing! As it is, it cannot give an adequate picture of God's 'Security Arch'. If it is to do this, we need to give it a soft inner lining – like the warm down under the wings of the mother hen that Jesus spoke of in Matthew 23:37. It also needs to be able to expand and contract, rather than being simply fixed. Gentleness and sensitivity are as much a part of God's 'Security Arch' as strength and durability. It both embraces us and gives us space. It is both soft and strong. It does not stand coldly and impassively by, but measures our needs and responds accordingly.

God wants us all to grow up within a structure like His 'Security Arch'. But we will only do so if our key nurturers, by being strong, sensitive, and reliable, manifest the qualities of the Arch. They must be able to take us in their stride – good or bad, easy or difficult – and to love us come what may. Only if they do this will we be sure that nothing that we can do or say will ever jeopardise the security that we have in God's love. To the extent that they fail to do this, Overload Bearing will inevitably become an integral part of our souls.

Fear is the key

Like Love Earning, Overload Bearing is rooted in fear. But it is fear of a different kind. With Love Earning our fear centres on our own performance. We fear most of all that we will lose love if we fail in our responsibility to be lovable. Our attention is focused on **what we are**, and on making sure that we match up to expectations. The issue is whether we can merit that love. But with Overload Bearing our fear is not centred on ourselves and our responsibilities, but on other people's capacity to love us. The shortcomings of love sources are the issue. We sense that they are struggling in different ways to be there for us. We fear that they may fail us as a source of security if we do not help them. Their being there for us and loving us is the foundation of our lives, so we feel compelled to try to prop them up. The alternative seems to be a terrifying free fall into space.

So fundamental is our need to have the floor, walls, and roof of God's 'Security Arch' under and around us that, where our parents show signs of struggling to provide these, through their weaknesses and the flaws in their characters, we get sucked inexorably into helping them. We do this so spontaneously, and from such an early age, that we become locked into the habit of shouldering other people's responsibilities long before we reach adulthood.

This is not all. Because of the way that our key nurturers represent God to us, we project their limitations onto Him. In our hearts we set limits on His ability to go on loving and supporting us, and, worse still, on His ability to cope with His responsibilities generally as creator, sustainer, provider, and protector. Rather than seeing Him as He is, and confidently leaving Him to take care of His responsibilities, we see Him as being like His human agents. We do what we can to prop Him up too, and to fill any gaps in His ability to 'be God'!

In Overload Bearing, the message that our souls speak to our spirits is something like this:

> 'There is no all-wise, all-mighty, all-coping being in control of this world and all that there is in it. Such a God as exists needs my help if the things that matter are to get done. I must carry the world with Him.'

Overload Bearing is rooted in a misguided ministry to failing nurturers. It is always accompanied by deep anger, disrespect, fatigue, and anxiety – anger at being robbed of childhood by premature adult responsibility; disrespect for those who failed us; fatigue because the task is too onerous for us; and anxiety because of what failure may mean.

The early stages of Overload Bearing can take two forms. It can be actively helping adults to fulfil their responsibilities, or it can simply be suppressing or denying what we are in order to take pressure off them. Both are done to relieve crucial stress on them. Examples of the former are looking

Figure 31

after depressed or drunken parents, or younger siblings, or being responsible for housework. Examples of the latter are bottling up our stronger emotions (see Chapter 14 – 'Emotion Storing'), or conforming to expected patterns of behaviour.

Figure 31 on the previous page shows what life can feel like for Overload Bearers.

Sarah's story

Sarah was 45. She had grown up with a violently angry father – though to outsiders he presented a calm Christian exterior. His anger, which often caused him to lash out physically, could be set off by a variety of triggers. These resulted in outbursts that were explosive, and terrifying to Sarah and her sisters. Worst of all, they were not always predictable.

She wrote:

'When I was a little girl, I tried to keep the home as peaceful as possible. So I was always very quiet and good. I felt that my father's angry eyes followed everything that I did, watching my every action. As a result it was always very tense being in the same room as him. I believed that our lives were in danger if I made a wrong move. Arousing my father's anger was potentially disastrous, and I never knew when the next explosion might come.'

For Sarah, her father's outbursts of anger were like the tremors of an earthquake, threatening to shatter her 'Security Arch'. As an adult, she was constantly tormented by the thought that she may have made a crucial mistake. 'Did I say the right thing? Did I do the right thing?' she would repeatedly ask her closest friends. She never knew for certain whether her 'performance' in any situation involving other people had been good enough. She felt as if she was always being watched and judged. Singing in the worship group at church, or simply eating a meal with friends, could make her so anxious that she actually trembled and shook.

When Sarah was a child she had lived in dread of her 'Security Arch' disintegrating. Though she had since grown up, and her universe had widened, the little girl inside her was still haunted with the possibility of this happening. Huge amounts of subconscious attention and energy went into preventing this.

Sarah's story is more extreme than most. Usually the signals that draw us into Overload Bearing are of a subtler nature. With Linda's parents, for example, there were no explosions. Nonetheless she sensed the daily strain they were under, as they struggled to cope with the presence of her awkward grandfather, and did what she could to avoid adding to the pressures on them. Even our imaginary little boy in the last chapter, by helping his father to cope with the pressures in his life, was sowing this condition into His soul.

Overload-bearers take on general managership of the world! Where others need help, overload-bearers cannot resist volunteering. Saying 'No' is something they can almost never do. They also find it difficult to delegate. Overstressed church leaders love them, as do the idle. But those who want to grow and to take on more responsibility find them obstructive and frustrating. Because of their fear of what will happen if they let go, they deny others the opportunity to prove that they too have the ability and skills to get things done.

Love-earners, through their desire to please, tend to elevate others and make them feel important. Whereas overload-bearers, through having to do too much themselves, tend to look down on others and make them feel small.

Overload Bearing, like Love Earning, is difficult to detect, but for different reasons. It looks and feels for all the world like sacrificial serving. For this reason it is a sin condition that is actually prized in Christian circles! We assume that the toll it takes is just worthy sacrifice and suffering. Its results are seen as acts of love. But the fear that drives it, and the way it undermines others, go unnoticed.

Overload Bearing denies us Christ's 'easy yoke' and 'light burden'. Instead it places a constant, excessive weight on our shoulders. As in Sarah's case, this can sometimes be crushing.

It is not difficult to see the overtaxation and under-resourcing that characterises all sin conditions at work in Overload Bearing. Overload-bearers constantly do other people's work for them. At the same time their judgments about the inadequacies of others, including God, close them off from receiving. Their 'inner child' tells them that God is as inadequate to meet their needs for security unaided as were their own human nurturers. They look to others for less than they can be, and to themselves for more than they can comfortably shoulder.

Laying our overload down

Release from Overload Bearing comes when, deep down, we see God as the strong and resourceful Father that He really is, and allow **Him** to be our 'Security Arch'. It also comes as we let people around us show us what they can do. This means, with God's help, one by one identifying and surrendering all our false judgments about Him. Only as we do this will we begin to let go, step back, and let Him be God. It means identifying and giving Him our false judgments about people too. This will enable us to see them through God's eyes, and to give them the space that they need to sink or swim, as they wish, rather than elbowing them out with our fear-driven overactivity.

Chapter 14

Further Common Conditions

The three other sin conditions which widely affect people are each a natural progression from the three that we have already outlined. They show the same basic processes at work. So we can deal with these quite briefly.

These conditions are:

- Emotion Storing
- Controlling
- Love Substituting

Emotion Storing

Emotion Storing is suppressing or bottling up feelings inside ourselves.

Each and every one of us are acutely feeling beings. We are capable of experiencing a whole range of different feelings. There is never a conscious moment in our lives when we are not feeling something. Feeling is simply a fact of our lives.

Our ability to feel is God-given, and serves two important purposes. Firstly, it enhances our enjoyment of life. Feeling is to living life, what taste is to eating. It brings what we experience to life inside us. Secondly, our ability to feel generates actions. These may range from brief, automatic facial expressions – such as frowns or smiles, which do no more than reflect what we are feeling – to conscious, willed courses of action.

There is no need to list here all the different emotions that we can experience, or the actions to which they may give rise. What matters is understanding that we generate emotions all the time. To live is to feel. We sometimes talk about 'feeling nothing'. But even then we are feeling something.

Emotion Storing takes place when, rather than letting our emotions run their course, we habitually suppress what we feel.

If having feelings is natural and good, why do we sometimes suppress them?

Emotion Storing is the result of Love Earning and Overload Bearing. We do it either to avoid rejection ourselves, or to spare others the full weight of what we are, and what we are feeling. The false judgments about God and other people that underlie those conditions also underlie Emotion Storing.

There are many reasons why key nurturers may not be able to accept us, emotions and all. They may mistakenly see anger as bad behaviour and disrespect, or tears as weakness and self-indulgence. They may be too insecure or proud to face the reality of what we truly feel, especially when it represents an indictment of their parenting.

Everyone stores emotions from time to time, but it is a particular speciality of the British, who widely see the expression of certain emotions as a sign of weakness, ill-discipline, or bad manners. When we call someone 'emotional' this is often a criticism in itself.

Of all the emotions, anger is perhaps the most frowned upon, and so the most heavily suppressed. As a consequence, stored anger is often the last emotion to surface in the healing process.

Like Love Earning and Overload Bearing, Emotion Storing is about pandering to our sources of love and security. These are vital to us, so we make sure that we do it well. But Emotion Storing has its price. Feelings contain a force of their own, like electricity. If given expression, and allowed to run their course, they serve their God-given purpose, and are dissipated in the process. If suppressed, they accumulate and grow in strength, inwardly overloading us. If and when they are finally released, their effect can be explosive and destructive. Stored in any quantity they can be seriously damaging to others as well as to ourselves. Emotions that are allowed to accumulate inside us inevitably force their way out in messy and unpredictable ways – today's people becoming the innocent victims of yesterday's feelings.

Charlotte's story illustrates the startling power that some stored emotions can contain, and the unexpected ways in which they can be triggered.

Charlotte was a Christian woman in her mid-forties, and a respected pillar of her local community. She was a headmistress, a wife, and the mother of two grown-up children. One day, quite out of the blue, she discovered that her husband was having an affair.

It was only natural that she should have felt hurt and angry. But what shocked her was the power of her reaction. She seemed to turn into a wild animal. She became uncontrollably violent – at one time throwing bricks through the windscreen of her husband's car, and having to be restrained by the police. When she was calm, an immense sense of sadness and loss seemed to churn around inside her. She soon became unable to concentrate properly on her job, and was forced to take leave of absence. She felt ashamed and perplexed at her inability to cope with her circumstances in a dignified way.

During our sessions with Charlotte, it emerged that the pattern of aggressive outbursts alternating with overwhelming sadness, that overtook her when she discovered her husband's infidelity, was the result of a lifetime of Emotion Storing. The course of her life, from the moment of her conception, meant that she had every reason to be both very angry and very sad. Conceived and born out of wedlock, and unwanted, she had been put up for adoption by her natural mother. Her adoptive parents were cold and disciplinarian. Rather than offering her the extra affection and acceptance that she needed, they subjected her to a barrage of strict religious rules. The message they gave her was that provided she was 'Miss Perfect' all would be well. They also made it clear that she should be grateful that they had given her a home. All this left little room for any show of anger or tears, which she believed would have been seen as being difficult, self-pitying, and ungrateful.

So, despite all the injustice she had suffered, Charlotte felt compelled to keep her perfectly legitimate feelings of anger and hurt locked away. And there they remained, growing with every new injustice and wound that a sinful world inflicted on her, until the day she discovered her husband's affair. At this point they swept over the forces of restraint that had held them in check. Like a tornado, they swirled around inside her, and then burst out.

Charlotte's story shows what stored anger can do. But even subtler feelings, like resentment, bitterness, or jealousy, can wreak their own special kind of havoc, if we go on storing them. The same is true of sadness or grief. Quite apart from what they do to our souls and spirits, all these emotions, when stored, can stress our bodies too, and so affect our physical health. We have already mentioned arthritis, but there is ample evidence that many other forms of physical ill-health, such as circulatory problems, heart disease, and cancer, can be brought on by prolonged Emotion Storing.

Emotion Storing has three other main side effects. We can use the example of stored anger to explain these.

Emotions are a gift from God. But, as the Bible tells us, stored emotions become sin. Thus there is no ban on feeling angry and showing it. God gets angry at injustice and wrong. When we do the same we simply manifest His nature, which is to react robustly towards evil, and thus to counter it. Ephesians 4:26 tells us, however, that we should express anger, and not hold on to it. If we do, then our ability to feel and to express righteous anger does not serve the purpose for which it was given to us – as a wholesome response and antidote to wrong. Instead, by misuse, it changes quality and becomes sin. As such, its first effect is automatically to obstruct the channels between us and God – cutting us off from the benefits of unhindered relationship with Him.

Secondly, it becomes a pollutant to all our relationships, leaking out to sour them. And finally, it drains us, through the energy that we use to keep it suppressed.

Most of us who store emotions are neither aware of how much emotion we are storing, nor of what this is doing to us. This is partly because our Emotion Storing is such a long-standing habit. It is partly, too, because the effort required to suppress emotion is only stepped up gradually – with each successive wave of emotion that we store. For many of us, it is only when we either erupt, or become so drained by this process that we do not have sufficient energy left to fulfil basic daily tasks, that we first become aware of the toll that Emotion Storing is taking on us.

Susan, who we have already met, provides a good example of this.

When she first came to see us, unknown to her, she was still holding on to all the painful feelings aroused in her as a child by an uncommunicative and remote father. Carrying these, and holding them down, had drained her. As sin, they had also cut her off in her deep places from God's resourcing power. The result was chronic fatigue, and a loss of any real sense of His love.

To help her to release her emotions, we encouraged Susan to pretend to write a letter to her father, and to explain her feelings about their relationship to him. What happened took her completely by surprise. Here is what she wrote:

'Dad.

It's a measure of my pain and love for you that even as I went to fetch the pen and paper the tears started to flow. Three lines and three tissues already. My love for you has been so great, and so constant, that I'm still trying to take in now the knowledge that the one man who meant the world to me has caused me so much pain as well. Though I in no way want to dishonour your name or memory, I see and feel now something of the pain you have caused me, albeit in ignorance.'

Susan went on to give her father specific examples of how, in his remoteness, he had fallen short of the standard of love prescribed under God's 'Double Agenda'. She told him how this had affected her, before finishing:

> 'I've spent so many years rationalising those things that, if it wasn't for the tears that keep flowing, I'd think I was making it all up. I don't understand, Dad. Though I can perhaps see your own upbringing clearly now, I still have this bewildering sense of betrayal – not only as a woman, but as a child. I needed you. I wanted you, and you weren't there for me. So now I cry, and cry, and cry again. Thirty three years on. The pain is still here.'

A few weeks later Susan went to a Christian meeting at which a speaker referred to women 'who had been abused in the past'. She wrote this to us:

> 'I remember being vaguely aware of a huge well of sadness within. Slowly, it was as if my emotions were unfreezing, and the depression within began to rise, filling, it seemed, my entire being. I didn't think of myself as having been abused, but something triggered off inside of me, and, oh boy, did I cry. Howled. For what seemed like hours. It was as though that well of sadness and brokenheartedness had been uncovered and emptied out. I crawled to bed, too exhausted to think or speak or even feel.'

Readers will recall that, slowly at first, but very surely, Susan came into a completely new experience and understanding of God and His love. With this came joy, and a new supply of energy. Recognising and clearing out the emotions that she had stored inside herself was crucial to making this possible.

We have no doubt that some forms of ME are caused or contributed to by stored emotion. We have known some who have immediately come out of extreme fatigue after a powerful release of deep-seated emotions.

If we are ever to release the emotions that we have stored, we need to know that far from rejecting us if we do, God will actually welcome it. We need to realise that we have His permission to do so. Seeing His perspective on our upbringing, and knowing that, when we first experienced them, the feelings that we have subsequently stored were a perfectly legitimate response to the quality of love that we experienced, is a giant step in this direction.

Linda, who we also met in Chapter 3, acted on God's permission and did this. Like Susan, she too was taken aback by the force of her emotions. But, after our sessions together, she was able to write to us and testify to the releasing effect that this had:

'I had a list of the things that I felt angry and hurt about against my mother and father. What I was not at all prepared for was the depth of emotion I experienced. Almost from the start I began to cry. Not to sniffle. These were loud sobs. It felt as though all the deepest hurts, the feelings of neglect and loneliness, started to surface. They came from very deep down. I'd removed the lid and the release overwhelmed me. It also felt as if the person crying was the child I was when I first experienced the pain.

I was also very angry. Being able to feel that anger and express it was also a great release for me. Until that point I was still locked into the childish pattern of wanting to please my parents to make them love me.'

Once again, repentance is our gateway to freedom from Emotion Storing. We need to repent – not of having feelings in the first place, but of our failure to express them. This does not mean just being sorry, and trying not to do it again, but also expressing and releasing what we have stored. If we do not, any forgiving will be premature and wrong.

Whether we are aware of them or not, we all start the healing process with some 'I-owe-you-and-you-owe-me' feelings inside us. These can often be intensified by discovering just how we have been let down. Yet, while our heads say 'Forgive!', our hearts will often say something else. They know instinctively that to do so before giving expression to our stored emotions would simply be to put the lid back on them, and so to bind ourselves to the past. We should listen to them.

There is practical help with releasing stored emotions in the section entitled 'Preparing to forgive' in Chapter 16.

Controlling

Despite what its name might suggest, this condition is not primarily about exercising power over people or events. It is first and foremost a defence.

In Love Earning a person's aim is to draw as much 'love' as they can from others. In Overload Bearing it is to prop up sources of security. Both have to do with getting as much of what we need out of people as we can. There is a kind of control involved in these conditions, but in both cases its aim is to obtain something. Controlling as a condition has nothing to do with getting anything out of anyone. Instead it is about keeping other people and events where we want them. It is about arranging the landscape of life around us, including people, into a configuration that makes us feel safe. It is about keeping sources of threat at a safe distance.

Like all sin conditions, Controlling works in some ways. But like all sin conditions it also robs us of the full life. Once again, it impales us on that two-pronged fork – under-resource and overtaxation.

The under-resourcing comes because, through false judgments based on past relationships, Controlling puts limits on true interaction with God and the world around us. The

overtaxation comes from the extra effort involved in continually assessing the landscape around us, and in working to
control it.

Freedom from Controlling means coming to a place where
we are simply ourselves. This means being open, honest, and
sometimes vulnerable, and trusting God to order the landscape around us for the best. This, in turn, comes with an
ever greater and deeper experience of His healing and
strengthening love.

The repentance that frees us from Controlling is letting go
and letting God.

Love Substituting

God has made each of us with a basic, all-consuming need to
be loved. He is the ultimate source of this love – though, as
we have seen, He sometimes uses human channels to bring it
to us. If, through their failures and our own barriers, we
do not absorb enough proper love, we will inevitably seek
ungodly substitutes. In fact, until we begin to know God's
unearnable, unconditional love in our souls, **everything we
do is in some way linked to our need for love**. If the real
thing is not available, we locate and pursue substitutes. Love
Substituting is trying to meet our legitimate need for love
through these ungodly substitutes.

Love Substituting stems from the false judgment either
that godly love is not available, or that it will not satisfy our
needs. Both of these judgments are based on misinformation
about what God and His love are really like.

We love-substitute when we try to meet our basic, legitimate need for God's love by: looking to human love; having
sex outside Christian marriage; engaging in fantasy love,
sex, and self-stimulation; overeating; drinking alcohol or
coffee for their chemical effect; taking drugs (medical and
hallucinogenic); acquiring material possessions, status, or
power.

God may show us His love by giving us people and things
to enjoy, but none of these will in themselves fulfil our

deepest needs. Pursuing love-substitutes, like all other sin conditions, overtaxes us. By turning our spiritual receivers away from the real thing, it also ensures that we continue to remain under-resourced.

Because of our absolute need for God's truth-bearing love, and because human love always falls short, we start to love-substitute very early. We therefore especially need the Holy Spirit's convicting work if we are to root this condition out. Only giving God all our love-substitutes, and so clearing the way for Him to meet our every need in His chosen way, will finally free us from this condition.

Chapter 15

Depression

'Why are you downcast, O my soul?
Why so disturbed within me?
Put your hope in God,
for I will yet praise him,
my Saviour and my God.'
(Psalm 42:5 NIV)

What is depression?

Depression defies any neat definition. It has different ingredients in each case, and can vary greatly in intensity. What we can say, however, is that depression always brings feelings of lowness, together with a loss of mental and physical energy. It can also include feelings of worthlessness, isolation, and hopelessness – detracting seriously from our ability to fully participate in life.

The term 'depression' is often too loosely used. We frequently describe ourselves as being depressed, when all we mean is that something has happened to make us feel momentarily pessimistic or discouraged. Certainly depression includes negative feelings, and events may sometimes seem to trigger or worsen it. But there is much more to true depression, as we define it, than a passing reaction to events.

Where depressions occur, they tend to last and to recur, as if they have a life of their own. They do not automatically lift just because life around us looks up, nor do they affect only pockets of our lives. Instead they persist, regardless of circumstances, and colour our entire outlook. At their worst, they can become so immovable, and make everything look so hopeless and black, that life no longer seems worth living.

What causes depression?

Depression is not in itself a sin condition. Rather it is the result of the sin conditions that live inside us. This is why we deal with it separately, and after sin conditions.

In Chapter 2 we described the soul. We summarised it by saying that, in a sense, we each live in two worlds: the real world outside ourselves, and the inner world of our own souls. Depression occurs when our souls surround and oppress our spirits with a sufficiently negative or burdensome picture of life, and when the under-resourcing and over-taxing effect of sin conditions, which are woven into those souls, begins to wear our spirits down. Particular events may worsen our souls' picture of life, and so increase the extent to which they oppress and drain our spirits. These events may be the straw that breaks the camel's back. But it is in the overall world-view of our souls that our susceptibility to depression lies. And this is formed over many years, and goes very deep.

This explains why depression clings on, and why, unlike a mere mood, it has an indifference to events around us. It also explains why no two depressions are ever quite the same. Each experience of depression is coloured by the way in which the sufferer's soul is made up (by their unique reaction to a unique life experience), and by the inner picture of life that it carries.

We can (provided it is true!) tell someone in depression that we know **something** of what they must be feeling. But we can never say that we know exactly how they feel. To do this our spirits would have to have lived in the inner world of **their** soul. And they can never have done this.

What makes a person susceptible to depression?

Because depression is rooted in the soul, its seeds are sown in our soul-building years.

The opposite of depression is radiance – the radiance seen in Jesus. We saw in Chapter 2 that this had its source in His perfectly formed soul, and in the quality of His relationship with God. Far from imprisoning or oppressing His spirit, Jesus' soul kept Him fully open to God, and free to shine. It did this because it was formed in a perfect nurturing environment, which had God and His pure love at its centre.

The key to radiance is a soul like Jesus' – made in heaven. But for us the key to building such a soul is receiving God's truth-bearing love into ourselves in our formative years, through the medium of God's 'Double Agenda' for our parents and other key nurturers.

By contrast, every failure to receive God's truth-bearing love into our souls sows some of the seeds of depression. The less we are shown about what God is like, and about His unconditional love and power for us, and the more we are blocked in fulfilling our potential and the purposes for which we were created, the more we will build an inner world that is cut off from Him, that oppresses and drains the spirit, and that pushes us closer to the downward spiral to depression.

None of us were perfectly nurtured. All of our souls are in some way affected by sin conditions, with their under-resourcing, overtaxing effects. On the overall scale of spiritual health, we are all somewhere between the perfect radiance of Christ and the blackest depression. In this sense we are all depressives. It is simply that in most of us under-resourcing and overtaxing have not reached a serious enough level to become of concern, or detracted sufficiently from our spirits' ability to sustain us for us to be labelled 'depressed'.

[Incidentally, we see ME as being closely related to depression. Both, in our experience, are symptoms of sin conditions living within a person, though they each have a different effect on us. Whilst depression primarily crushes our spirits, ME tends to exhaust us physically.]

Release from depression

Understanding depression, its roots within us, and how these can be removed, is of special importance – not just because of what its onset so powerfully says about the scarcity of God's life-giving truth in our deepest places, and about how different our souls are to Christ's, but also because of the misery that it causes so many of us.

Just as it is for all other forms of un-Christ-likeness, the antidote to a depressive tendency is the truth-bearing love of God, penetrating the deepest levels of the soul. Depression is a wretched affliction. Especially for those of us who have experienced it ourselves, the more severely it affects a person, the easier it is to feel great sympathy for them. Yet those of us who suffer depression must ultimately go through the same healing process as everyone else. We must choose to forgive, and then to surrender the sin conditions that underlie this tendency, if we want to become permanently free of it. There is no other route to a soul that blesses and frees the spirit, rather than crushing it.

No one is keener than God to fill the depressive's soul with the truth it needs. The same David who speaks in Psalm 51 of a God who 'desires truth in the inner parts', also reminds us in Psalm 139 of a God who knows us thoroughly, and so is able to put His finger on every barrier inside us that keeps that truth out. Because of this He waits eagerly to hear from the depressive the words David wrote at the end of that Psalm:

> *'Search me, O God, and know my heart;*
> *test me and know my thoughts.*
> *See if there be any wicked way in me,*
> *and lead me in the way everlasting.'* (Psalm 139:23–24)

In the end, transformation is choice and action – for those of us who suffer depression as much as for anyone else. But (exceptionally) in the case of those of us who suffer it severely, and especially those of us who hit rock-bottom, this may have to wait. We are all capable of receiving some reviving truths, just as we are. And we may need first to do nothing more than to let go and let God's accepting and understanding love come to us in those ways in which it **can** immediately find access. Then, when sufficient mental and physical energy have returned, we will be able to embark on the active process that will bring about a full and permanent cure.

Deep down, those of us with a depressive tendency lack an understanding of the unquenchable, unconditional nature of God's love. The more severe the tendency, the worse our understanding. Because we are also chronic love-earners and overload-bearers, and locked into working hard to earn the things that God wants to give us for free – like a sense of self-worth, wellbeing, and security – doing and achieving seem crucial to us.

The onset of depression means that we are already running low on resources, but, rather than rest, our instinct as depressives is to work even harder to try to hold off the depression, the negative feelings it produces towards ourselves, and the sense that things are grinding to a halt. The effect is the exact opposite to the one desired. If it has not already done so, this pattern will inevitably bring us to a standstill, and we will not have the energy or desire to play our part in the healing process. Depressives are convinced that all love has to be earned. Our first need is to realise that God's love is different. We need to be shown a love that understands and accepts us as we are, and that we do not have to earn at all. Only when we have grasped this, will we be motivated and energised to do the work needed to fully open the doors of our souls, and to let that love right in.

Dorothy's story provides dramatic evidence of what can happen when God's love reaches previously closed areas of the depressive's soul.

It was whilst I (Richard) was at theological college, preparing for this ministry, that I met Dorothy. The students at the college had decamped for the weekend to different parishes across the country – to put into practice what we had been learning in the classroom. I particularly remember that time, because healing Dorothy was not the only way that God intervened supernaturally.

Contrary to all the normal rules then applying in conventional church circles, I, a single man, found myself allocated to stay with Dorothy, a single mother, for the weekend! On our first evening together I learned that she regularly had to make arrangements for her nine-year-old daughter to be looked after, whilst she was treated in hospital for debilitating depression. Her visits lasted, on average, for three months of every year.

With my interest in healing, I went to bed pondering Dorothy's illness. I strongly suspected that it had its roots in her past history, and that God could deal with it by changing the information in her soul. At that point I knew nothing of her history. A few simple questions might confirm my diagnosis, and open the door to change. Yet I was reluctant to delve so quickly into this issue with a single woman whom I had only just met.

I went to bed in this quandary. As I closed my eyes, a simple image appeared inside my eyelids. I saw two babies wrapped in blankets. Each blanket was different. One was made of silver foil, the other of angora wool. The Holy Spirit seemed to be telling me that the two blankets represented two different types of upbringing. The silver foil blanket represented an upbringing in which all the practical necessities of life were supplied, but no more. It lacked the special, warm, cherishing, and accepting love that God intends all of us to receive in our natural families, if we are to grow up not only physically, but also spiritually and emotionally, resourced. The angora wool blanket represented just such a quality of love – a 'luxury' love that goes far beyond just providing for our practical, physical needs. As I thought about this, God seemed to be telling me that the baby in the foil blanket represented Dorothy, and that this absence of 'luxury' love was the cause of her depressions.

Looking back, it is obvious that God gave me this information because He wanted to use me to heal Dorothy. Yet I was still reluctant to raise the issue with her. However, I could find no peace nor fall asleep whilst I resisted God's prompting. I finally resolved that I would share what He had shown me, and the next thing I knew was that it was morning!

At breakfast I told Dorothy about the picture, and asked if it meant anything to her.

It did indeed mean something to her! In fact it perfectly described her childhood. She told me that she had been born outside marriage; that her natural father had disowned her; and that her mother had placed her in an orphanage, because she felt unable to bring Dorothy up on her own. She told me that she had lacked for nothing in terms of food, clothing, a roof over her head, and a basic education, but that all had been delivered to her in a cold, businesslike way. She knew nothing of the warm, personalised, 'luxury' love that in God's eyes is every child's birthright.

My picture convinced Dorothy that God wanted to work in her life. It showed her that He was a God who was capable of understanding what she really needed. She accepted that, if He **was** love, what had happened to her must have broken His heart more than anyone else's. This helped her to suspend some of her false judgements against God, and to open the deep places within her, which had been closed since early childhood, to His healing touch.

Together we asked the Holy Spirit to come and minister to her. Over the minutes that followed, I watched her facial expression change gradually from one of blank emptiness to one of deep joy. 'I am with Jesus,' she said quietly at one point, but nothing more.

She later told me that almost immediately we had begun to pray she had been taken back, in all but body, to her childhood at the orphanage. She had then enjoyed a day like none she had ever known as a little girl. Jesus had come and taken her out – just her – for a picnic. She found herself seated with Him in a golden meadow, wearing what to her was the most beautiful party dress she could ever have imagined. Jesus had given it to her. This was the centrepiece of a kind of cherishing that she had been denied in real life.

This brief, powerful, and perfectly measured injection of love put an end to Dorothy's bouts of illness. A few minutes 'face to face' with Jesus and she was never to feel depressed again. Her regular stays in hospital became a thing of the past. His presence energised her spirit, and lifted out all the darkness and weight in her soul. He reached the little girl inside her, who until then had felt deeply alone and insignificant, with a message that changed her forever: the message that **her Creator knew all about her, and that she really mattered to Him**.

Just being depressed can be bad enough. As time goes by, however, depression can become more and more frightening. It can feel like being trapped in a maze, and unable to find a way out.

There is always a mix of sin conditions underlying depression. But equally, as Dorothy's story and mine (Richard's) show, Jesus always knows how to break its back. With His guidance, and by His power, there is no reason why any Christian who is experiencing it should not very quickly find themselves on an upward spiral to freedom and radiance.

We say 'break its back', because just as one sin condition in the soul leads to others, and together they cut us off from God and overwhelm our spirits, so also one touch of God's healing and freeing love can, at a stroke, start to bring the whole complex sin structure inside us tumbling down. The Holy Spirit gladly makes use of even the smallest of openings. One shot of the well-targeted truth that He brings – to the little boy or girl inside us – can dislodge crucial misinformation at the root of all six of the sin conditions that we have described. It can bring a new understanding of God and of His unconditional love. As a result false judgments about Him can become true judgments, and in no time Love Earning, Overload Bearing, Emotion Storing, Controlling, and Love Substituting can all begin to fall like dominoes.

PART FIVE

PUTTING THEORY INTO PRACTICE

Chapter 16

Transformation –
a Step by Step Guide

'Do not merely listen to the word, and so deceive yourselves.
Do what it says. *Anyone who listens to the word, but does not*
do what it says, is like a man who looks at his face in a mirror
and, after looking at himself, goes away and immediately forgets
what he looks like. But the man who looks intently into the
perfect law **that gives freedom**, *and continues to do this,*
not forgetting what he has heard, **but doing it –**
he will be blessed in what he does.'
(James 1:22–25 NIV)

We have now completed our overview of the process of
transformation. We have seen how un-Christ-likeness
becomes rooted deep within us, how God can make us new,
and what we must do to make it possible for Him to do this.

To leave it there, however, would be to stop short of our
central purpose in writing this book: to enable those who
read it to **actually experience change**.

By following a few simple, practical steps, those whose
individual stories we have told, and many others, have
opened themselves to profound change. This chapter sets
out these steps.

If we truly want change, there is no reason why we too
should not begin to experience it right now. If we do, we

have two options: we can either go straight ahead and put these steps into practice on our own, or we can find someone with appropriate gifting and insight in this area to help us.

How do we know which is the best option for us?

'DIY' or expert help?

For the practical steps that follow to be an effective door-opener to the healing work of the Holy Spirit, we need by now to have a good grasp of:

1. The kind of love that God meant us to receive throughout our early years.

2. The ways in which our key nurturers have fallen short of God's expectations.

3. The sin conditions that 'live' within us, as a result.

To be real and effective, forgiving and repenting must be specific.

If we are unclear in any of these three areas, then we should consider asking for help. For some of us, finding our way through the healing process can seem like being an explorer in totally uncharted territory. An experienced guide may make all the difference.

A key element in the healing process is freely expressing our true feelings about the past. For some of us, this may mean being completely ourselves for the first time. Sometimes we can do this on our own. However, giving expression to long-buried feelings can be unnerving. Until now the 'inner child' in us will have gained much of its sense of acceptance and security from being nice to (and about) love sources. So the prospect of being brutally honest for the first time can be a daunting one. We can feel extremely vulnerable – instinctively fearing rejection. Having someone else there, who understands the kind of challenges that face us, can be crucially affirming. It can also comfort and steady us when particularly painful or traumatic memories come to the surface, as they sometimes do.

These are just some of the reasons why we may want to consider having the help and support of a caring counsellor. Nonetheless, for those of us who feel that we would like to go ahead on our own, here are the steps.

Steps to transformation

Step 1

Find a quiet, comfortable place, where you will not be interrupted or overheard. Allow plenty of time, as well. This process cannot be rushed.

▶ **Identifying who we need to forgive and what for**

Step 2

Come before God, and ask Him to bring to your mind, one by one, everyone you need to let go of by forgiving.

Step 3

Turn back to the 'Double Agenda' diagram on page 125 in Chapter 7. Using this diagram, and the contents of that chapter generally, ask God to show you every person that has fallen short of their God-given responsibilities towards you, and that you need to hand over to Him in this way.

Make a list of these people.

Step 4

Against each person on your list (and using the same diagram and chapter), note down the specific wrongs that **you feel** each has done to you. These may be things they have done or things they have failed to do. They may have been ongoing, or they may have been isolated incidents. They may have mattered a great deal, as you see it, or been comparatively trivial.

► Identifying our sin conditions

Step 5

Ask God to show you everything about yourself that He wants you to surrender to Him.

Our sin conditions mostly stem from choices made a long time ago. They will usually have become so much a part of us that, without God's help, they are impossible to see.

Step 6

Using your list of those you need to forgive, and remembering that we all get our picture of God from our key nurturers, especially our parents, ask Him to show you every way in which you have falsely judged Him to be like them.

Write these judgments down.

Keep an open mind, giving the Holy Spirit time to show you all the ways in which God, as you picture Him deep down inside you, differs from the God of the Bible.

For example, do you really believe that He is **always**:

- unreservedly pleased to see you?
- longing for fellowship with you?
- in tune with your every thought?
- interested in your concerns?
- attentive to your prayers?
- on your side?
- completely forgiving?
- fully in control?
- strong, resourceful, and wise enough to fully meet your every legitimate need in the best way possible?

In short, has He up to now been a God who is **always there for you**, both as almighty God and as the best friend we could ever wish for?

Step 7

Ask God to show you all the other sin conditions that have resulted from your false judgments about Him.

Write these down.

Another look at Chapters 11–14 may help you here.

Step 8

Ask God to show you any individual wrong thoughts and actions, that have resulted from your sin conditions, and that He specifically wants you to bring to Him for His forgiveness.

It is not necessary to recall every sin we have ever committed! At the same time, it is not enough just to name our sin conditions. We do need to surrender these, but we also need to recognise, confess, and be forgiven for some of the specific sins that have resulted from them. These are just as much our responsibility.

Be open to the Holy Spirit and take your time. He will cause just as much detail as is necessary to flow into your mind.

For example, Love Earning may have led you to give your own God-given rights low priority, and to suppress your true desires and feelings. It may also have led you to deny Jesus for fear of unpopularity. Similarly, Overload Bearing may have caused you to wrongly take responsibility for particular people or situations. Love Substituting may have led you to look to one or more of the things listed in Chapter 14, in place of the all-fulfilling love of God.

Write down all that God shows you.

▶ Preparing to forgive

Step 9

Place a chair (no taller than the one you are sitting on) a few feet in front of you, and facing you.

Our first goal here is to forgive those that have failed us as nurturers. It is to let go of them, and to commit them once and for all to Jesus, so that He can see justice is done, and we can be free of our cold war with them.

In a moment, one by one and in your mind's eye, you are going to put each of the people that you have listed into that chair. You may have been a victim of their sin in the past, but it is important that you do not see them as if you are still beneath them and controlled by them. You must see them as fellow human beings and sinners. You must rise up, look them in the eye, and tell them, with the confidence that comes from knowing that your point of view is valid in God's eyes, what they have done or failed to do, and what you are forgiving them for.

Before we actually pronounce forgiveness, **it is vital that we have the opportunity to tell each person just how we *feel* about what they have done, or have failed to do, and how this has affected us**. Remember, if we do not, we will simply put a lid on our feelings. We will remain negatively tied to them and to the past, and the Holy Spirit will not be able to create the clear ground within us that He needs if He is to fill us with Himself. If we do not allow what is inside us to fully express itself, saying we forgive will simply seal the past in. Instead of being a mechanism of release, it will just be an exercise in gritting our teeth and trying to forget.

There will be time enough, in the months and years that lie ahead, to feel and express warm feelings towards all those we put in the chair today; time enough to be tolerant of their weaknesses and failings. What is crucial now is not to hold back, but to give the 'inner child' within us his full right to be heard.

When we are ministering to people, we call this prelude to forgiving 'Talk Back'. This is because for many it is the first opportunity that they have had to talk back freely and openly to those who have been in authority over them.

As we saw when we discussed stored emotions, the ability to feel is God-given. Every child should be given a clear message that it is okay to express his feelings, even when these are critical of those in authority over him. But often, because of their insecurity, pride, and need to control, nurturers withhold this permission. This means that many of us grow up with a lengthy backlog of complaints that we have yet to register with our key nurturers. If we are to truly put the past behind us, these need to be spoken out, and the feelings associated with them expressed.

Step 10

Put your first choice in the chair.

Start with the person that you feel has wronged you most.

When we turn our minds to those we need to forgive, this person will normally be the first one that we think of anyway.

However keen we are to do it, true forgiving is always an act of will and an effort. Those who have wronged us most can be the hardest to forgive, and our 'Talk Back' with them is often the most painful and tiring. It can, therefore, be tempting to put off facing them. But these are all reasons why forgiving them is best dealt with while we are fresh and our resolve is at its strongest. Also, the greater the need to forgive, the greater is the release and relief when we have done it, and the easier it becomes to deal with the others lower down our list.

Step 11

Face your first choice. Close your eyes, if this helps you to focus on them, and on what you want to say to them. **Then, in a clear and firm voice, tell them all you noted against their name in Step 4, and what you feel about it.**

This is not an exercise in character assassination. Those who need our forgiveness are not all bad. They may have got certain things wrong – some of them very important, but there will usually be much else for which we continue to love and appreciate them. Because of this, and especially where parents are concerned, many find it helpful to begin 'Talk

Back' by thanking a person for who they are, and for all the things they got right.

Again, don't rush, but take your time. Make sure you unburden yourself completely. Small things matter to children. Anything that has mattered to the little boy or girl inside you has mattered to God.

► **Forgiving**

Step 12

Forgive them, and release them to God.

Here is a form of words that expresses the key elements of forgiving. You may wish to repeat it as it is, or just to use it as a guide:

> '[Name], these things that you have done (or failed to do) **have** mattered. They **have** affected me. I have told you exactly what I feel about them. There is no denying them. There is no excusing them. But I do not want to hold on to you any longer. Instead I want to receive the healing that I need from Jesus.
> I want to give you to Jesus, so that He can hold you to account for your sins, and ensure that justice is done on my behalf.
> So, [Name], I now forgive you once and for all, and I release you to Him.'

Step 13

Go back to Step 10. Repeat the process for each person on your list.

When you have released every one, take away the chair from in front of you.

Postscript to forgiving

What of those we have forgiven? Do we need to forgive them face to face?

As far as our own healing is concerned, the answer is: no. In terms of benefiting them, the answer is: maybe.

To explain this, we need to look at how our forgiving benefits the person receiving it.

When we truly forgive someone, then the whole way we relate to them and feel towards them automatically changes. We no longer carry, and therefore project at them, all the ingredients of unforgiveness – the demands, the desire to repay or to get even, and the disappointment and resentment that goes with these drives. So, though they may not instantly be able to pinpoint what we have done, they will immediately experience a difference in us, without our having to say anything at all.

Forgiveness may be spoken out, but a new attitude can convey it too. This is what matters most. There may come a time when a person who has sinned against us in the past specifically asks us if we forgive them. In the meantime, our new attitude will make it easier for them to do this.

Spoken forgiveness can complete a reconciliation between us and someone who has wronged us. It can also relieve them of regret, guilt, and the fear of being confronted by us for what they have done. However, the crucial factor is timing. Words of forgiveness are called for only when it is clear that a wrongdoer will receive them. It is important to be sensitive to signs that this is so, and to be ready to say them, but no more. If we speak out forgiveness to a person who is not ready to hear it – either because they are ignorant of what they have done, or because they are unwilling to accept responsibility for this – they will not be able to receive the grace, the release, or the hand of friendship that it offers. It may even be counterproductive.

✤　✤　✤

If you have put Steps 1 to 13 into practice, you have now completed perhaps the most difficult element of your part in the healing process. You may have found it unexpectedly demanding. You may even feel quite drained. So, here are two suggestions to help you to press on and finish what you need to do:

1. Remind yourself that getting this far has actually been, from start to finish, a work of God's Spirit. It may have demanded a lot of you – spiritually, emotionally, and physically. But it is He who has shown you what to do, and enabled you to get this far. And He will help you to complete your part in the process.

2. If it helps, take a break now. It doesn't matter how long this is. What is important, however, is that you complete the rest of the Steps whilst the information that you have assembled is still fresh in your mind, and meaningful.

▶ **Surrendering our sin conditions**

Step 14

Quieten your heart, and be conscious of God's presence.

Then, in a clear voice, give God everything that you listed under Steps 6, 7, and 8.

Don't make any excuses, or try to persuade God that there were special circumstances that somehow make your short-comings less serious. He already knows and understands every ingredient of your past history. He knows all the forces that have shaped you. Simply take full responsibility for the things you have written down, and tell Him that you are sorry for them all.

Here is a form of words that expresses the key elements of repentance. You may want to repeat it as it is, or just to use it as a guide:

'Loving, compassionate, and merciful Heavenly Father, thank you for showing me the truth about myself as You see it.

Thank you for showing me my sin conditions, and the wrong thoughts and actions that have flowed from them.

Thank you that You have done this because You want me entirely free of them, and of the sense of failure and guilt that goes with them, and because You long to take away every barrier between me and all that You are, and have to give me.

Thank you, too, for the discomfort that the awareness of my sin now causes in me, and the desire that this creates within me to surrender it completely to You without delay.

I acknowledge and accept full responsibility for all my sin, namely [all those things you wrote down under Steps 6, 7, and 8].

I am truly sorry for all my sinfulness. I now surrender it to You. Thank you that the blood that Jesus shed on the cross means that I can, at this moment, be forgiven and set free from all guilt and fear of punishment for what I have been, and what I have done.

I ask that, as an act of my will, and with the help of the transforming power of Your Holy Spirit, I may become fully and finally free of everything within my soul that is not perfectly Christ-like.

Where my sin has consisted of deep-rooted patterns of thought and behaviour, I ask that You strengthen me by that same Spirit, so that my repentance may not simply be words spoken once. Help me to make it a deep and continuing act that keeps open the way to Your work of cleansing, freeing, and healing me to the very deepest levels of my being.

I now gratefully receive Your complete forgiveness for all that I have confessed to You, and I accept Your offer of continuing forgiveness and help for the future, as I battle on with new resolve against my own sin, the world, and the Devil.'

God's word assures us that:

> *'If we [freely] admit that we have sinned and confess our sins, He is faithful and just ... and will forgive our sins ... and [continuously] cleanse us from all unrighteousness...'*
>
> (1 John 1:9)

Now pause, and allow the truth that God has forgiven you to sink in.

▶ Receiving the Holy Spirit's healing

It now only remains for you to allow God to reach and touch the places within you that need His gentle but powerful healing love.

He may want to begin to do this immediately, in the kind of supernatural way that we have described. If so, it is most important that you give Him the opportunity He is looking for.

Step 15

Sit or lie in a position that is the most comfortable and relaxed for you, and that enables you to let go of all control.

Step 16

Close your eyes. Forget your physical surroundings and all your worldly concerns. Focus on God, and open your mind and your heart to Him.

By all means ask God for the healing that you want. But remember, He already has the fullest possible picture of what you need, and may have a different order of priorities to yours. What is most important is that you let your whole being say:

> 'I am completely Yours, Heavenly Father, Lord Jesus, and Holy Spirit to touch and to speak to in any way that You want to, and when You want to.'

Step 17

Relax in God's arms, and go with the flow of whatever the Holy Spirit chooses to do.

Allow plenty of time for God's Holy Spirit to do or to say all that He wants to, before going on to the next Step. You will know instinctively when He has finished what He wants to do at this time.

Step 18

Allow yourself time to absorb and enjoy, and perhaps to record, what the Spirit of God has done.

This is important.

God may, for example, have taken us back in time to minister to us. We may have become for a few brief moments the needy little boy or girl of the past, whilst He touched us in some special way with His healing presence. If so, then this will have been a precious experience. We should savour it, and not rush too quickly back to present-day realities.

Step 19

Express your gratitude to God for what He has done.

This can be done either out loud, or through a prayer spoken quietly within your own heart. Choose whichever of the two comes most naturally to you.

What if 'nothing' has happened?

Many who follow Steps 1 to 19, experience immediate and dramatic transformation. On top of the relief of forgiving others, and unburdening themselves of their own sin, they find Jesus coming to them by the power of the Holy Spirit, and touching them in a life-changing way.

It is only natural that we should want to experience immediate results. But this does not always happen. Sometimes our experience may be more like that of Anne, who we met in Chapter 4. She, too, followed these Steps without anything happening there and then. Yet it was only a short time before the Holy Spirit was ministering wonderfully and powerfully to the anxious, self-doubting little girl inside her.

We understand how hard it can be to have to wait for the healing that we are looking for. There have been many times in our own lives when we too have had to do this. So we hope that the next chapter, which contains advice for all our readers on going forward from here, will be of special help to those who find themselves in this position.

Chapter 17

The Way Forward

*'I am convinced and sure of this very thing, that He Who began
a good work in you will continue until the day of Jesus Christ –
right up to the time of His return – developing [that good work]
and perfecting and bringing it to full completion in you.'*
(Philippians 1:6)

For those who have followed the Steps in Chapter 16, and
experienced God touching their souls in a supernatural way,
we rejoice. It is understandable and right that they should
want to bask for a while in what He has done. But, even for
them, this will not be the end of the story.

Provided we are open to it, the process of change is one
that will continue, right up to the time that we go to be with
God. The principles that we have set out in this book are not
for 'once only' use. It is our hope that, under the Holy Spirit's
guidance, readers will apply them to their lives over and over
again, as they become aware of further healing needs, and
that each time God will use them to bring still greater
wholeness.

No matter how momentous any particular working of the
Holy Spirit in our lives may be, there will always be more that
God wants to do to change our souls. It is a wonderful and
exciting thing when we receive a powerful, supernatural
touch from Him, especially when it is the first time that this
has happened to us. But there will be others. And, anyway,

we should view such times as special, accelerated bursts of change in a normally more gradual process – through which we are becoming ever more whole, and through which our enjoyment of life is ever increasing.

God has a perfect plan for the rest of our lives. If we remain obedient and open to Him, as we have been in following the Steps in Chapter 16, that plan will surely be fulfilled. Remember, it is important not to try to impose our expectations and timescale on God. First, this will not help Him to work as He needs to. And second, it will lead to frustration, disappointment, and discouragement

One day soon we **will** receive the full extent of the wholeness that God has purposed for us in Christ. When this happens, the reasons for any delay will most likely become clear as well. In the meantime our task is to make sure that we do not succumb to any temptation to doubt or resent God. If we do, we run the risk of reversing the openness and expectancy that will allow Him to work as He wants, and of holding up the completion of His perfect plan.

Satan is a master at leading men to erect barriers between themselves and God. Some of us have worked hard and waited a long time to open the doors of our souls to God. It would be a tragedy if, having come so far, we were now to allow ourselves to be tempted to close those doors again, and to have any new found hope and expectancy taken from us.

Particularly if we have not yet received **all** the healing and change that we hope for at this time, the first thing that we should do is to secure the ground already gained – ready for the Holy Spirit's future working. We should thank God here and now for what **has** been accomplished, and commit ourselves to Him for what remains. He has seen every last detail of what we have done in obedience to His instructions. We can be sure that He will honour this, and will not let us down or disappoint us in the long run.

God works in His own perfect way and timing. We are each unique, and our own circumstances differ from everyone else's. So the way that He works in each of our lives is different. He never fails to fulfil His side of any bargain. If we give Him time and allow Him to, He will lead each of us forward into the full salvation that we are promised in Christ.

If God does not yet seem to have met your expectations for change, the prayer that follows may be especially important to you. It may help you to leave your needs in His loving, capable hands, and to wait upon His further working in your life with complete inner peace.

There will be some who read these pages at a time of great pain and discouragement. For some the desire for change may have become desperate, and still not have been fulfilled. Our hearts go out to them, and we say to them prayerfully, with Peter:

> '... *after you have suffered a little while, the God of all grace – Who imparts all blessing and favour – Who has called you to His [own] eternal glory in Christ Jesus, **will Himself complete and make you what you ought to be**, establish and ground you securely, and strengthen (and settle) you.'*
>
> (1 Peter 5:10)

Even if today's needs have been met, there will be others that present themselves in the future. Many of these will be linked to sin and sin conditions of which we have yet to become aware. If we are to deal with these, we shall continue to need the convicting work of the Holy Spirit to help us. Once again, co-operating with God will be key. For this reason, we too need to make sure that we stay open to Him, keep trusting Him, and expect Him to work.

It is our hope that the prayer below will be helpful to all who read this book, as they seek to maintain these attitudes, and so to preserve the access that God needs in order to be able to complete His work in them, and as they entrust themselves to His safekeeping for their onward journey through life to the full measure of wholeness that He has waiting for them:

'Loving Heavenly Father, I thank You for the wholeness that You have already brought me.

I commit myself to You for the healing and transformation still awaiting me.

I welcome the convicting work of Your Holy Spirit, and ask You to show me any unforgiveness or other un-Christ-likeness in my thinking, behaviour, or make-up that I still need to surrender to You.

Thank you that You know what still needs to be done, and that Your unshakeable word tells me that You, who have begun a good work in me, **will be faithful** to complete it. Thank you that You can be trusted absolutely not to let me down, and that You will lead me forward from here, if I allow You to.

Please continue to give me the faith to look forward, with an open, trusting, and expectant heart, to the work that You have yet to do in me.

Thank you that **You are God**. Amen.'

Now rest quietly on the promise of God's faithfulness. He **will** lead you forward.

Further reading

The purpose of this book has been to teach our readers enough to enable them to come into an experience of the deep-rooted radiance that Jesus bequeathed to every Christian. There are, however, two further areas that can have a direct bearing on whether or not we take possession of this inheritance. These are outside the scope of this book, because others have already given them excellent coverage. Nonetheless, we want to draw them to our readers' attention, in case they may wish to research them further for themselves.

These are:

- Deliverance from unclean spirits
- Release from the effects of generational sin

Deliverance from unclean spirits

Sometimes we can be held back from release into full, Christ-like wholeness by unclean or mischievous spirits that have made a home in us. These may have forced their way in through traumatic things that have happened to us, or we may have invited them in ourselves, through our own sin.

Unclean spirits are wicked spirit personalities – usually specialising in one specific form of sin or sickness. They can make a home inside us, and express their characteristics through us. In this way they can encourage and perpetuate different kinds of sin or sin conditions, and therefore **the entire structure of un-wholeness within us**.

For example, False Judging may be locked into our make-up by critical or accusing spirits; Love Earning by spirits of fear of rejection or fear of man; Overload Bearing by spirits of insecurity or control; Love Substituting by spirits of lust or addiction; and Emotion Storing by spirits of anger or grief.

If we have followed the 19 Steps to transformation, and yet not experienced the change that we were looking for, it may be (and we stress **may be**) that we are being denied this by indwelling spirits. If so, we will need to evict those spirits.

It is the Holy Spirit's work to pinpoint the presence of any indwelling spirits within our make-up. If we ask Him, He can be relied upon to do this. Where unclean spirits have affected us for a long time, it may only be in the lead up to being set free that we become aware that patterns of thought and behaviour that we have always assumed to be our own have, in fact, another source.

Any unclean spirits that do have a home in us can insist on staying only for as long as they continue to have rights that enable them to do so. Where these exist, they will have been given by our sin, or possibly by the sin of one or more of our forbears. (See the next section.) The sin in question may be a fresh one, or one committed years, or even decades ago. Sin conditions also give unclean spirits a right to stay. Once these have been removed through forgiving and repenting, the process of evicting the unclean spirits is relatively straightforward. Sometimes God delivers us sovereignly. This being so, indwelling spirits can sometimes put great pressure on us not to respond to the quiet promptings of God to deal with any unforgiveness or other sin that He is showing us.

What this means is that it is far more important to focus on God, and on being shown our own un-Christ-likeness, than it is to go pursuing unclean spirits. We have seen much time and effort wasted in this way. What really matters is that we play our part in the way that we have outlined already, **which gives us the keys to cleansing of the very deepest kind**. Once we have, deliverance from any unclean spirits may often be little more than a formality.

Although unclean spirits tend to have their own single specialities, they all have one characteristic in common. Like their father, the Devil, they are all habitual liars. Because of this, we must be sure that we look to God to tell us how, and how much (if at all), we are being affected by them. Especially if we are approaching this area on our own and for the first time, it is vital that we exercise careful discernment under God. **We cannot stress this enough**.

Unclean spirits adopt a variety of tactics to avoid being found out, and thrown out. On the one hand, when they sense that we are on their tail, they can temporarily switch off, and go into hiding. They can also go to great lengths to deny this whole area of Satan's activity, or try to mislead us into thinking that there is an entirely different cause for our problems. At the other extreme, they can step up their activity within us, in an attempt to overwhelm, confuse, and demoralise us. They can tell us, for example, that we are indwelt in all sorts of ways that we are not at all.

The hallmark of God's guiding is that it brings clarity and peace – even when it contains truth that we would rather not hear. The voices of Satan and his spirits, on the other hand, bring confusion and fear. We must be careful not to listen to them.

If you have not heard about unclean spirits before, you may want to get help. Alternatively, you may want to read some of the many helpful articles and books on this subject that are around at the moment.

A book that we particularly recommend is *Christian, Set Yourself Free* by Graham and Shirley Powell (Sovereign World). This is the most comprehensive, clear, balanced, and practical manual on unclean spirits that we have seen. It covers such topics as: what they are, how to discover whether they are affecting us, and how to set about evicting them.

There are also a selection of Christian resource centres that offer teaching in this area. One that we can recommend is:

> Ellel Ministries
> Ellel Grange, Ellel
> Lancaster LA2 0HN

They have branches in both the north and south of England.

Whether we get help or not, responsibility for dealing with any unclean spirits that may be affecting us lies ultimately with us. Where we are indwelt by unclean spirits, this is rarely because we have deliberately invited them in. Usually they have simply crept quietly in through doors opened by our sin or by trauma. We are all sinners, and vulnerable, so this can happen to any of us. We must not allow pride to come between us and getting free of unclean spirits, any more than we would allow it to prevent us facing our sin and dealing with that.

Release from the effects of generational sin

The Bible tells us that some sins can adversely affect a person's children, grandchildren, and subsequent generations of their family, as yet unborn. This means that, through no fault of our own, we can inherit specific imperfections and weaknesses. These may include a propensity towards certain kinds of spiritual or physical ill-health.

There are a range of serious sins that can produce this generational effect. The books of law in the early part of the Old Testament list many of these, the leading example being the worship of false gods, which is referred to in the Ten Commandments.

This is not an unduly complicated area, and again there is plenty of sound teaching about it available. The relevant chapters in Derek Prince's *Blessing Or Curse: You Can Choose* (Word Publishing) are one place to start.

The good news is that complete release from the effects of generational sin is available through the Cross. We obtain this essentially by forgiving our forbears for those of their sins that have affected us in this way; by allowing the consequences of those sins to be reaped henceforth by Jesus on the Cross, rather than by us; and by receiving the restoring ministry of the Holy Spirit.

Getting further help

If the contents of this book have struck a chord within you, but you feel that you need help with applying them to your own life, and do not know anyone with the appropriate gifting, then you are welcome to write to us.

Our address is:

PO Box 2449
Blandford Forum
Dorset DT11 9YP

We will be pleased to do whatever we can to help you. Anything that you write will be kept in the strictest confidence.

Epilogue

Passing It On

*'His intention was the perfecting and the full equipping of **the saints** ... [that they should do] the work of ministering toward **building up Christ's body** ... [that **it** might develop] until **we all** attain oneness in the faith and in the comprehension of the full and accurate knowledge of the Son of God; that [**we might arrive**] at really mature manhood – the completeness of personality which is nothing less than the standard height of Christ's own perfection – the measure of the stature of the fullness of Christ, and the completeness found in Him.'*
(Ephesians 4:12–13)

God wants all His children whole

As we discover the keys to personal transformation, and put them into practice, we begin to experience real change for ourselves. We also become carriers of a message that urgently needs sharing with others in the Body of Christ.

The passage above from Ephesians reminds us that Christ's Body on Earth is built up by our sharing with others what we ourselves have received. The God who wants **us** whole and happy, wants the same for all our Christian brothers and sisters. He loves **them** as well! Furthermore, He knows that a strong and Christ-like Church will be the most effective at drawing unbelievers into their own relationship with Him.

The message of the Bible, underlined in this book, is that we can each become like Jesus the man. He had an incalculable impact on the lives of all He met. So can we. But turn this around, and it means that our own continuing un-Christ-likeness has implications way beyond just our own personal happiness and health. It impoverishes not only the Body of Christ to which we belong, but ultimately our entire nation.

A law to remember

Jesus underlined God's Law of Sowing and Reaping, and Paul warned us:

> *'Do not be deceived ... whatever a man sows, that and that only is what he will reap.'* (Galatians 6:7)

This law is as real and as certain in its operation as the Law of Gravity.

We sow and reap what we are. To the extent that sin reigns in our make-up, and expresses itself in our thoughts and actions, we will each continue to reap a bad harvest. This will affect not only our own working, playing, and relationships but, through those relationships, the lives of others as well.

Many of us long for God to change the circumstances around us. We direct much prayer at them, when all the time it is *us* that need to change, if we want to sow and to reap a better harvest.

Perhaps one of the greatest examples of good being sown in this country's long history is seen in the heroism of the sixteenth century Christian martyrs. These few men and women stood up resolutely for truth, in the face of great evil. Like Christ, they had the faith and courage to put holding fast to what they believed was God's will before their own lives.

We know from contemporary accounts that those who witnessed their deaths were profoundly affected by what they saw. But what the martyrs sowed by their actions has meant that this country has reaped another, far greater, harvest. Ever since that time, ours has been a Christian country.

One of those martyred was Latimer, who was burnt at the same stake as Ridley. As the flames consumed them both, he was heard to say:

> 'Be of good comfort, Master Ridley, and play the man. We shall this day light such a candle, by God's grace, in England, as I trust shall never be put out.'

Roman Catholicism, whose official teaching remains as antithetical to the central truths of real, biblical Christianity as it ever was, has become firmly entrenched in almost all of central and southern Europe. In its failure, thus far, to capture this country, we see just how great a difference even a few Christians can make, when they are securely 'rooted in', and 'founded on' God.

That counterfeit 'church', whose prime aim has always been to hold power over the lives of ordinary men and women, is once again, stealthily but steadily, gaining ground - both through its hierarchy here in Britain and through the European Union, by which we are increasingly governed. In many other, perhaps more obvious ways, too, the forces of darkness are marching across our desperately backslidden, yet still Christian country. We need only to open our eyes, and look around ourselves, to see just how rampant they are. It is harder and harder to freely and openly live out our beliefs. And being Christian feels increasingly like being an alien in a foreign land.

All in all, the need for strong, whole men and women of God, who will stand up, and speak out, for Christian values and beliefs, and sow again for this country's future, may be greater today than it has been at any time since the sixteenth century itself.

The best people to publicise the life-transforming aspects of the Gospel are those of us who already have some experience of these working in our own lives. To highlight just how badly the Body of Christ is suffering for lack of knowledge in this area, and to encourage our readers to share what they are learning, we want to end with a brief snapshot of some of the wider consequences of our continuing deep un-Christ-likeness.

A people of pretence

We have seen that imperfect nurture meeting our fallen natures has two main effects. These are inner starvation, and inner defence barriers. Together they mean that we are needy, and yet prevented from receiving.

We have also seen how, through Love Earning, we try to buy both yesterday's and today's supply of love – particularly from people. Pleasing them, in order to win their 'love', is often our priority. We have seen how, on top of this, Over-load Bearing causes us to spare others the full weight of what we really think and feel.

These sin conditions make us people who instinctively give low priority to being our true selves. Instead, we major on being what we think other people want us to be, and what will least impose on them. And all the time we keep our vulnerable places carefully hidden. The result is that artificiality, superficiality, and a lack of true, connecting fellowship are everywhere in our churches. Not only are our own true needs unmet, but we are also pathologically unable to speak out, or to constructively receive, the very truths that would challenge us, as a people, into change.

Genuine love relationships are **the** uniting force. They allow for real communication. Through them we can be known, understood, and accepted. They create, as a matter of considered and informed commitment, bonds between people that cannot easily be broken. Without these we may be able to produce an appearance of unity. But this will be of little real value. Relationships that are essentially about mutual mollycoddling, and often little more than skin-deep, may hold up during times of comparative tranquillity. But when disruption, pressure, or attack befalls a fellowship, their superficiality is exposed for what it really is – something that holds us carefully and safely apart, rather than truly together.

Only heart-to-heart relationship can provide unity that runs deep, and that can withstand such times of testing. A unity of convenience that is built around the dictates of our sin conditions – carefully constructed so as not to reveal or seriously impinge on the real, yet damaged person inside us – can never do this. It is only ever precarious, building up false confidence between us, and papering over divisions and a lack of real communication, rather than enabling them to be faced and removed.

At times genuine self-expression can be messy and disruptive. But in a mature, secure, and therefore forgiving fellowship it is never fatal to the bond of unity. So long as sin conditions are allowed to rule in so many of us individually, true unity will continue to elude the fellowships to which we belong.

For the vast majority of those to whom we have ministered, our counselling room has been the first place where they have ever been able to be open, real, and completely themselves. The people we see are just the tip of the iceberg – some of the very few who are grasping their right to radical change. Their openness, honesty, and willingness to face the truth invariably bring them great reward. Yet they bring evidence, too, of the poor state of relationships within the wider body.

It is our privilege that people feel able to be themselves with us. But how much better it would be if the same level of honest interaction were taking place across the fellowships to which we all belong. Its effect on our relationships, our unity, and our witness would be enormous. Without real transformation by the power of the Holy Spirit taking place we will never come into these blessings.

A taking people

Some years ago I (Richard) was attending a Sunday morning service at our lively local charismatic fellowship. We were being given one of those uncomfortable sermons that must have been repeated in countless services in churches up and down this country through the years.

The speaker was exhorting us to greater efforts, both within the fellowship and for Christ in the world. With undertones of rebuke that were veiled yet unmistakeable, he was listing all the benefits that God had given us in Christ, and telling us of the ripe harvest of souls that was waiting to be reaped all around us. The Church, he was reminding us reprovingly, was 'the only club that did not exist for the benefit of its members'. [Incidentally, we think it does! Although we should naturally want non-believers to share that benefit as well.]

In common with many others, our fellowship was made up of a few keen and hard-working people, and a majority who by and large seemed content to freewheel. The effort to get more out of this latter group went on continuously. Yet little ever seemed to change.

My first, self-righteous inclination was to unite with the preacher in criticising the laggards. Instead I found myself wondering why repeated sermons like this were necessary at all. Why, I asked myself, is it so hard for leadership to get people in this fellowship to do the things that for them, as Christians, should flow naturally?

To my surprise, an answer came. Almost as if a voice had spoken to me, I felt God say:

'It is because so many people in this fellowship are **in permanent deficit**. They can't give, because they need to receive.'

This, of course, is just how it is for so many of us. The inner effect of having taken in insufficient food for nurture during our formative years is that it makes us, individually and together, a people who are in deficit. We may have a good intellectual grasp of the Christian ethic of giving. We may have resolved to put this into practice. We may even look like givers. But what will always prevail in the end will be the deeper drive to get our own lifelong hunger for love met. It will make us natural takers, rather than givers.

God gives out of fullness. His love for us is an 'overflow' activity. He wants our loving to be the same. That way we will always have enough for ourselves, and to give away, and so give naturally and willingly. Giving out of deficit works badly, if at all. It is at best a continuous struggle, at worst impossible. Yet this is what vast swathes of the Body of Christ are trying to do.

We have described love as 'an accurate measure and supply of another's needs'. For as long as we are inwardly in deficit, the voice of our own hungry 'inner child' will always vie with our desire and ability to assess and supply the needs of others accurately. The deprived child inside us will continue to insist on its rights. Those we try to love will not actually have their true needs discerned and met. They will sense this, though they may not be able to put their finger on quite why.

Our ability to hear God will also be impaired.

In many quarters within the Body of Christ today, great emphasis is being placed on the importance of each of us listening to God. Hand in hand with this, we are being encouraged to step out in faith in the things that we believe He is saying to us and, where appropriate, to share them with our fellowships.

As a result 'words of knowledge' – short pieces of information, which are seen as given by the Holy Spirit to one member of a fellowship to enable him to help or to guide others – are increasingly commonly spoken out, in the context both of church services and one-to-one ministry.

There are, at any given time, three 'voices' audible within us: the voice of God, the voice of Satan (frequently spoken to us through evil spirits), and the voice of our own needy selves. This means that there are two strands to hearing God's voice correctly: picking it up, and distinguishing it from the other two. This complicates our hearing Him, and so hampers our ability to receive all that He wants to say to us by way of acceptance, affirmation, instruction, guidance, and encouragement.

The more whole we are the more the other voices diminish, and the clearer God's becomes. In the meantime, it can often be the voice of the little boy or girl inside us – wanting approval, insecure, angry, and so on – that wins out. We can be as much their spokesperson as God's.

This deficit syndrome and its effects are widespread – not just amongst the rank and file of the Church, but also amongst its leaders. Here it has perhaps its most damaging consequences. Leaders are there to serve and to give to their flocks. But, by definition, a person in deficit cannot purely give. His 'serving' will always be tainted by his own needs, often to the point where it is not true service at all.

Many of us will know the experience of joining fellowships hoping to find them a source of refreshment and resource to fuel us for our daily lives, only to find them yet another drain. This is because many congregations up and down the country are more about leaders ministering to their own needs, than about their ministering to the needs of their flocks.

Every Sunday, for example, thousands say nice things to their pastors about their sermons, not because their own lives have been changed by what they have heard, but because they sense their pastors' need to hear these things. Running a successful church is many church leaders' chosen antidote to low self-esteem. Up and down the country many Christians, from organists to organisers, from servers to sidespersons, from performers to mere pew-fillers, find themselves, in a whole host of ways, sucked into this hidden agenda. Their own Love Earning and Overload Bearing tendencies may make them only too willing to fall in with this ungodly scheme of things. But in doing so they become part of a vicious circle, in which deficit meets deficit, and ultimately no one benefits.

Jane's experience was just one of many like it. Brought up in a Christian home, she was nonetheless deeply needy. Not only had her parents failed in many ways to follow God's 'Double Agenda', but she was also one of six children. This greatly diluted what little love there was available to her. Her young life had been a constant struggle to press buttons that attracted attention and approval, and gave her some sense of self-worth. Academically and at home she became a 'model' daughter, from a young age accepting levels of responsibility way beyond those that God intended for her.

In the years before we first met her, Jane had experienced a run of events, including a stillbirth, that would have taxed anybody. But their effect was magnified by her own Love Earning and Overload Bearing. She tried to cope with them perfectly, on her own, and without burdening others. This brought her to near collapse.

What Jane then needed more than anything else was to rest and be built up. A healthy fellowship could have allowed her this. But hers, from the pastor downwards, was itself deeply in deficit. Facing several personnel crises of its own, it presented her with nothing but demands. She was already in a key role and contributing far more than she comfortably could. She desperately needed to receive. But all the fellowship offered her was more and more to do.

The answer, though drastic, was simple enough. She needed to withdraw. But to Jane that was anything but simple.

A break might have been what she needed, but how would the fellowship manage without her? More important still, where would it leave her in their eyes? Nobody seemed to understand. In one direction, it seemed to her, lay a complete breakdown; in the other, and just as terrifying, the prospect of being rejected and bringing the world crumbling down around her.

Jane's story had a happy ending. She came to understand the conditions that affected her soul, and the pressures these placed her under. Through the healing work of the Holy Spirit, recognising and reaching down to the insecure little girl deep inside her, she came to know by experience that God's love was the only love that really mattered, and was free and unlimited. She also realised two more things: first, that her happiness was as important to God as anyone else's, so that what others might think of her was irrelevant in the face of God's love for her; second, that God knew and could shoulder the needs of all those around her. These truths set her free to let go and to find the space that she needed in order to regain her strength.

The facts may not always be the same, nor the predicaments so severe, but Jane's story represents a scenario that is repeated many times over within the Body of Christ in this country. Everywhere, Christians whose most pressing need is to receive find that they are asked to give instead. Our fellowships should be places where we can be ourselves, have fun, and be healed and built up. They should leave us happier and stronger. Instead, they often just add to the pressures on us. God's way, which is to give to us so that we can give to others from surplus, rarely operates. Faced with a people 'in permanent deficit' who are reluctant to give, yet widely unaware of why this is so, Church leaders habitually resort to spiritual arm-twisting. They tell their congregations that all giving is necessarily an effort, or try to make a virtue of giving from deficit by calling it 'sacrifice'.

An unanchored people

God is love. Paul prayed that Christians might become *'rooted and grounded in love'*. He prayed that we would all come to that unshakeable inner anchorage in God that only the inwardly transforming work of the Holy Spirit can give us.

At the beginning of this book we drew attention to the depth, strength, and closeness of Jesus' earthly relationship with God. This made Him immovably strong in the face of unparalleled opposition, and was the foundation of the huge impact that He had on the world.

The most important benefit of inner transformation is that it brings us ever more of this same quality of relationship with God. It brings home to our deepest places an ever clearer picture of God. The more real He becomes to us, the more He becomes the foundation of our lives – our one and only source of security.

To feel secure is one of our most basic needs. We want to be confident that day by day our own vital interests, present and future, and the interests of those we care about, are in safe, proactive hands.

Jesus said that if we want our basic daily needs met we must:

> '...*seek for first of all* [God's] *kingdom, and His right-eousness [His way of doing and being right].*'
>
> (Matthew 6:33a)

We must give expression to Christ within us, without reservation. If we do this, He says,

> '...*all these things ... will be given to* [us] *besides.*'
>
> (Matthew 6:33b)

This is His prescription for us, if we want to ensure that our own interests are taken care of. 'You focus,' He says, 'on fulfilling your Christian destiny. Do all you can to live out your calling – loving me, loving yourself, and loving your neighbour as you go – and I will take care of everything that matters most to you, including your personal needs.'

Despite this, for many of us the priority is seeking to meet our personal needs and those of the people who depend on us, both emotional and material. Sin conditions see to this. False Judging, in particular, gets in the way of our being able to do as Jesus says. It prevents us seeing God as He really is, and so trusting Him to fulfil His side of the bargain. This is especially true where human providers failed to perceive and meet our needs, or worse still, by reason of early death or divorce, were not there at all.

Where we prefer to depend on ourselves rather than God to provide for us, then the whole direction of our lives is affected. The decisions that we make, and that determine where we go and what we do, are hijacked by our inability to trust God's promise.

Many we know have changed direction, or even career, not because of God's call, but out of fear. Their upbringing and education have taught them to be self-sufficient, rather than to look to God.

God can, of course, work round our weaknesses, or even make use of them to bring about His ultimate plans. But there are times, too, when the wrong pulls within us can delay or defeat His full purposes for our lives, and diminish the quality of those lives.

Some tell us that a time is coming when God will *'shake all nations'* (Haggai 2:7). Others believe that that time has already arrived. All around us old sources of security are crumbling. More and more families are breaking up. The concept of a job for life is fast disappearing. Whole economies are collapsing. There has perhaps never been a time when the need to be thoroughly secure in God has been as great – not only if we are to save ourselves a rough ride, but also if we are to point others to the Rock.

In the late 1980s, an Iranian Christian called Mehdi Dibaj was imprisoned by Islamic Fundamentalists because of what he believed. On trial for his life, he was held in prison for nine years. Awaiting his fate, he wrote this to his persecutors:

> 'I am a Christian, a sinner who believes Jesus has died for my sins on the cross, and who, by His resurrection and victory over death, has made me righteous in the presence of the Holy God. The true God speaks about this fact in His Holy Word, the Gospel. Jesus means Saviour "because He will save His people from their sins".
>
> Jesus paid the penalty of our sins by His own blood, and gave us a new life – so that we can live for the glory of God, by the help of the Holy Spirit; be like a dam against corruption; be a channel of blessing and healing; and be protected by the love of God.
>
> In response to this kindness, He has asked me to deny myself, and be His fully surrendered follower, and not fear people even if they kill my body, but rather rely on the creator of life, who has crowned me with the crown of mercy and compassion, and who is the great protector of His beloved ones, and their great reward.
>
> I would rather have the whole world against me, but know that the Almighty God is with me; be called an apostate, but

know that I have the approval of the God of glory – because man looks at the outward appearance, but God looks at the heart. And for HIm who is God for all eternity nothing is impossible. All power in heaven and on earth is in His hands.

The Almighty God will raise up anyone He chooses, and bring down others, accept some and reject others, send some to heaven and others to hell. Now because God does whatever He desires, who can separate us from the love of God? Or who can destroy the relationship between the creator and the creature, or defeat a heart that is faithful to His Lord? He will be safe and secure under the shadow of the Almighty! Our refuge is the mercy seat of God, who is exalted from the beginning. I know who I have believed, and He is able to guard what I have entrusted to Him to the end, until I reach the kingdom of God – the place where the righteous shine like the sun, but where the evil doers will receive their punishment in hell fire.

It is now 45 years that I am walking with the God of miracles, and His kindness upon me is like a shadow. And I owe Him much for His fatherly love and concern. The love of Jesus has **filled all my being**, and I feel the warmth of His love in every part of my body. God, who is my glory and honour and protector, has put His seal of approval upon me, through His unsparing blessings and miracles.

The God of Daniel, who protected his friends in the fiery furnace, has protected me for nine years in prison. And all the bad happenings have turned out for our good and gain – so much so that I am filled to overflowing with joy and thankfulness.

It is our religious duty, as long as the door of God's mercy is open, to convince evil-doers to turn from their sinful ways and find refuge in Him in order to be saved from the wrath of a righteous God, and from the coming dreadful punishment. Jesus Christ says, "I am the door. Whoever enters through me will be saved." "I am the way, the truth, and the life. No one comes to the Father except through me." "Salvation is found in no one else. For there is no other name under heaven given to men by which we must be saved." Among the prophets of

God, only Jesus Christ rose from the dead. And He is our living intercessor for ever. He is our Saviour, and He is the Son of God. To know Him means to know eternal life.

I, a useless sinner, have believed in His beloved person, and all His words and miracles recorded in the Gospel. And I have committed my life into His hands. Life for me is an opportunity to serve Him, and death is a better opportunity to be with Christ. Therefore I am not only satisfied to be in prison for the honour of His Holy Name, but am ready to give my life for the sake of Jesus my Lord and enter His kingdom sooner – the place where the elect of God enter everlasting life, but the wicked go to eternal damnation.

May the shadow of God's kindness and His hand of blessing and healing be upon you and remain for ever. Amen.

With respect. Your Christian prisoner. Mehdi Dibaj.'

Nothing tests the strength of a man's security in God like the threat of imminent death. We quote this letter at length because it provides such an outstanding example of our potential to become fully anchored in God, and of the security that this brings.

Mehdi Dibaj, like George Muller, had been a Christian for many years, but it need not take long for God to become our true source of security.

During the course of his journey from being a Minister in John Major's government to a prison cell, Jonathan Aitken came into a living relationship with Jesus. The speed with which he became anchored in God was shown by his reaction to being charged with perjury and held in a cell at Chelsea police station. Describing this experience later, he said:

'This should have been a time of deep despair. The worst day of my life. Not so. For I had such an overwhelming sense of God's presence in the cell with me, that I was at peace.'

We can all know this same security in Jesus. Despite this, many Christians never come to such a place this side of the grave.

The signs are that we may be entering the end times, when a tide of ungodliness of every kind will increasingly swirl around us. If so, it is more important than ever that we are like lighthouses anchored on rocks. If God's children cannot stand firm above the raging sea, but rather are like small boats tossed and battered by each successive breaker, then they will neither endure with dignity, nor witness with any force to the truth about God. For as long as our souls are not filled with the reality of God, and so not truly anchored in Him, this is how we will be.

An ineffectual people

In His Sermon on the Mount, Jesus taught that Christians are to be:

> ' . . . *the salt of the earth* . . . [and] . . . *the light of the world.'*
> (Matthew 5:13–14)

He wants there to be a bite and penetration to the way we interact with others. As salt preserved meat in biblical times, so we are to keep the world spiritually fresh. As light dispels darkness, so we are to cut into the sinful thinking of those around us. In the very way we live and breathe, we are supposed to present a constant challenge to those around us.

In the same teaching, Jesus warned that we would become good for none of this if we lost our saltiness, or shrouded the light that was within us.

Love Earning and Overload Bearing overpoweringly force us to fit in with other people, and to avoid rocking the boat. The more pervasive these conditions, the feebler is our ability to be channels of challenge. We can neither confront others, nor stand aside and let God do it Himself. Our instinct is to please and to pamper.

Add to Love Earning and Overload Bearing a False Judging that sees God as a soft touch, and the result is, in many situations, a complete paralysis of the call on all of us to 'stand up for Jesus'.

The national press recently reported the findings of a survey conducted for the General Synod of the Church of England. In it, ordinary parishioners were asked both what animal the Church should be like, and what animal it was actually like. Some suggested that it should be 'like an octopus, with its tentacles extending into all areas of the community'. Others chose a lion, because it is 'an animal whose voice is heard'. In contrast, most saw the Church as actually being like a mole, because it is 'mostly under-ground and in the dark'. And some drew parallels with the ostrich, which sticks its head in the sand, or the chameleon, which is always changing its colour to blend in with the background!

It appears, then, that many of us are not only falling far short of what we should be, but know we are as well. Only when our souls are filled with a powerful sense of how big God is, and of His love for us, will we be freed from our fear of what people may think of us and stop shielding others from the hard truths that they need to hear.

A shrinking people

An important indicator of our wholeness is how fruitful we are in winning souls to Christ. Effective evangelism must always include an ability to challenge, but most importantly it is simply an expression of overflowing love. When he meets this, the unbeliever will always encounter a love that is empathetic and has his interests at heart. But, for many, to be 'evangelised' is actually to be on the receiving end of the neediness of individual Christians. What looks like witnessing may really be trying to gain approval, or to win an argument, or to notch up a conquest, or to control, for example. Whatever the underlying motive, the result will always be an evangelism that lacks the most winning aspect of Jesus' own approach to the lost – a heart of pure love for God and for the individual in question.

God can still work through the Christian who is in deficit, but their condition must inevitably affect their spontaneity, openness, and winsomeness, and hence their fruitfulness. It will also affect their stamina as an evangelist. Evangelism that is need-driven will struggle to keep going consistently in the long term. Deep down we resent having to earn love, whether through evangelism or anything else. It makes our activity a strain and a chore.

Evangelism that comes from fullness lasts. The Christian who is *'filled and flooded with God'* must evangelise or burst. He simply can't help loving the lost, so he will continue to reach out.

An empty-handed people

Christian counselling is a rapidly growing industry. This phenomenon no doubt represents the response of a sincerely concerned group of people to an explosion of spiritual, emotional, and physical ill-health in our society.

Frank Johnson, a former Editor of *The Spectator* magazine, recently wrote in his column in *The Daily Telegraph*:

> 'Counsellors are always saying that we must "come to terms" with this or that: with divorce, redundancy, alcoholism, acne. Most of us, however, have no wish to come to terms with these undesirable things. We want to get over them.'

True to Johnson's view, a nationally known Christian counsellor, when asked for her advice on how to deal with a husband with an uncontrollable temper, replied: 'Your GP should be able to refer him for anger management courses.'

Jesus never taught people to 'come to terms with' or to 'manage' their sin conditions. To those who were willing to submit to His lordship, He brought transformation. He did not send them away merely equipped to cope with their spiritual, emotional, and physical problems, but free from them.

As a result of what they either experienced themselves at first hand, or saw happen to others around them, the people who encountered Jesus the man enthusiastically passed on a life-changing Gospel.

We have already said that no one is as effective a preacher and practitioner of a transforming Gospel as the one who has personally experienced its life-changing power. He has a special faith to minister to others, and is living proof of what God can do. Others may see need and want to offer help, but without a personal experience of the transforming work of the Holy Spirit, what can they give of lasting value?

A former Chairman of the Accreditation Committee of the Association of Christian Counsellors, the body that governs professional Christian Counselling in England, once wrote in its Annual Review:

> 'It is amazing how easily hurt, rejected, and prickly Christian counsellors can be!'

It is true that no one is perfect, and that those of us who have known suffering are often the best people to help others. But it seems reasonable to ask, too: what solutions do such counsellors really have to offer? And how accurately can they hear in their spirits God's heart and mind for their clients? May not their desire to give counsel in fact be symptomatic of their need to receive it?

The psychiatric profession in this country has recently estimated that there are now half a million severely mentally ill people living here. It is said that one in ten of the population suffer depression. In Jesus we have all we need to bring real change to groups like this. If we preached a healing Christ with conviction, what a difference we could make. Yet, even within the Body, this message is muted.

For many months Michael was troubled by bad dreams and sleeplessness. These had their roots in deep wounds inflicted by a past relationship. He was a member of the largest, best-known Church of England fellowship in one of the largest cities in England. But the last thing that occurred to him was to look to Jesus for a solution to his problem! This aspect of the Gospel was simply not held out to the congregation. Instead, Michael sought help from other sources. He visited no less than five separate occult and New Age practitioners, who confidently advertised the help he wanted.

By the time we saw him, these 'healers' had multiplied Michael's problems. We were able to help him find the healing he needed – in Christ. But his story provides just one small example of what is happening all the time in a Church that knows so little about God's power to transform, or how to apply it to people's needs. The issue of homosexuality provides another. Here again the Church falls badly short, because God's power to transform is not part of its experience.

The Bible states in the clearest and strongest terms that homosexual orientation and practice are wrong. Yet faced with pressure groups arguing aggressively that homosexuality is not just a matter of conscious choice, but part of some people's make-up, the Church finds itself unable to argue for God's standards. God is changing homosexuals all over the world. Yet few in key positions in the Church seem aware of this. They have no experience of the transforming aspects of the Gospel in action. They do not know that God can always heal homosexuality, just as He can all other forms of deep un-Christ-likeness. The result is that, faced with the homosexuals' claim, they are forced into compromise or silence.

How different things could be if the Body of Christ were familiar with the Holy Spirit's transforming power. We could then preach and minister God's solutions as widely and boldly as the New Agers and occultists do theirs.

A vulnerable people

The further we want to go in God's service, the more important wholeness becomes. The greater our influence for good, the greater is Satan's interest in us, and the more destructive the weapons he brings to bear on us.

Wholeness at depth is the best defence against the schemes and attacks of the Evil One. Whether during His temptation in the desert or on His road to calvary, we see the value of this powerfully displayed in Jesus. Our own inner weaknesses, by contrast, provide Satan with many easy targets.

Some words spoken to me (Richard) by God in May 1994 explain the importance of being inwardly transformed to our effectiveness for God.

At that time, a number of those that we were ministering to were making great strides towards wholeness. However, far from finding everyday life the easier for this, they were often feeling more discouraged than ever. Some even felt suicidal. I asked God why. And this is what I believe He said to me:

> 'Satan watches people from the womb to the grave. He sees and participates in the damage that they suffer. He knows the weaknesses that this causes. He controls my Creation through their weaknesses. The "world" is thus widely under his control.
>
> When you become a Christian, I come to live in you by my Spirit. I am then, by your own choice, in control of your life. But when I seek to move you, or any Christian, forward within my plan, the more important the move, or the more damage it is liable to inflict on his empire, **the harder he shouts his lies at those weaknesses** which he has worked, through every evil source, including generational patterns of un-love, to create deep within people.'

In his first letter, Peter warns us:

> 'Be self-controlled and alert. Your enemy the devil prowls around like a roaring lion looking for someone to devour.'
>
> (1 Peter 5:8 NIV)

Discussing this verse in her classic bestseller *What The Bible Is All About* (Regal Books), Henrietta C. Mears puts it this way:

'The Christian life is like a jungle battle. Peter tells us who our enemy is. He is the Devil. His work is opposed to all that is good in this world. He is pictured as a roaring lion, seeking his prey. This adversary is cagey, appearing sometimes as an angel of light, at another time as a serpent, coiled for the strike. He is always seeking whom he may devour. He is watching **for the vulnerable spot, for the unguarded door to our hearts.**'

The American singer-songwriter, Julie Miller, sings about Satan that:

'He will tell you **any lie that you'll believe.**'

For each of us, Satan's lies are hand-picked to take account of our own particular background and make-up. When he deploys these, the mature adult in us may often hear nothing at all. But, deeper down, the still weak and vulnerable child inside us certainly does – word for word – and swallows every one whole.

Though, as Christians, we are ultimately assured of reaching heaven, by exploiting our weaknesses Satan can raise the stress, and lower the fruitfulness, of our journey there.

For example, so long as we are love-earners, he can play on our fear of rejection to make us anxious in our witnessing, or to stifle it completely. In the same way, so long as we are overload-bearers, he can burden us with responsibilities that are not ours. And so on...

Additionally, any one of our sin conditions may provide a foothold for unclean spirits, whose prime mission is to wreck our Christ-likeness, and to rob us of the full life.

An easily exploited people

Receiving all the different ingredients of God's food for nurture, through the healing process, does wonders for our self-esteem. As, through personal experience, we come to *'grasp . . . what is the breadth and length and height and depth'* of the love of Christ for us, we become less and less susceptible to being used and pushed around. Without this, however, we remain at the mercy of profoundly unbiblical teaching like: 'God first, your neighbour second, and you third'.

We British are experts at self-abasement – at the same time believing that this is somehow scoring us bonus points in heaven. We settle for a trade-off: many of our personal rights and needs are ignored, but in return we get the satisfaction of believing that both God and our fellow men admire us for our 'unselfishness'. There is, however, a high cost to this form of self-denial. Our own legitimate needs are repeatedly unmet, and conditions like Emotion Storing will ultimately result in ill-health. Our evangelism, too, suffers. Who wants to subscribe to a faith that will put them at the bottom of the pile!

When God's love reaches our deepest places, we begin to realise that this scheme of things neither makes sense, nor is God's plan. We come to see that we have legitimate, God-given needs, and an equal right, with everyone else, to have these needs met.

A driven people

The Christian life should be primarily about **being** with God. Our experience in the Body of Christ should be one of basking together in the sunshine of His active, continuous, and invigorating love. Such activity as there is should spring out of an overflow of Him from within us. Full of Him, and with our own needs already well satisfied, we should find ourselves living out our lives, and using our gifts and talents for the godly, pure, and often entirely altruistic purposes for which we were given them. We should move only on His command. A sense of peace and warmth, with an easy energy running through it, should characterise our gatherings, great and small.

Would that the reality of life in our fellowships always matched this ideal! Far from being places of abiding and recharging, many Churches are centres of what can only be

described as hyperactivity. In many, Sunday, though sup-
posedly set aside as the Sabbath, or Day of Rest, would more
aptly be named the Day of Exhaustion! Everywhere there are
fellowships where, on this day, members are offered: a
morning service; a fellowship lunch; some group activity,
like a walk, in the afternoon; a tea; an evening service; and an
evening prayer meeting or seminar! These events are
described as 'entirely voluntary', but members are 'encouraged' to take part in most, if not all of them. The more they
can manage, the more accepted and comfortable they feel
within their souls.

For as long as sin conditions continue widely to live within
us, this is how our fellowships will tend to be. Love Earning,
Overload Bearing, and Emotion Storing will all fuel overactivity at the expense of our true needs and feelings.
Our brothers and sisters may mistake such sin-driven
activity for 'good works'. In reality, it overrides our ability
to hear and to obey God's authentic instructions to 'go', to
'stop', or to 'wait'. These will be continually swamped by
fleshly impulses, which will also encroach on the ability of
others to find their own space with God. We ourselves will go
on feeling the weight of activity that flows not from fullness,
but from need; not from genuine enthusiasm, but from
fear.

For many, then, the Christian life will continue to consist
of expressing old drives in a new landscape. Whereas we may
once have been practised performers of the bad things that
our peer group was into, in order to be accepted by them, we
can now find ourselves 'acting like Christians' in order to
please our new peers. Fear of losing the new and better
quality of love that the Christian community generally holds
out to us, can have us working every bit as hard as we ever did
to earn love in the past – the prize now being that much
more desirable, and therefore that much more costly to lose.
We may have discovered a new and better world amongst
other believers, but Love Earning, Overload Bearing, and
suppression of our true selves will be working just as hard as
ever to hold this new world together.

Unbelievers have an excuse for all the time they spend trying to earn a sense of self-worth and security from other people. In a way, they must please others and pander to them. They know of no other love source. But we do!

If we are driven, we have yet to fully experience the supernatural love of God, reaching deep inside us, wiping out any deficit from the past, and meeting our present needs day by day. Nothing else can bring us the deep inner peace and contentment that will make us natural dwellers rather than compulsive doers. Only this can separate our doing from our need to feel loved and secure, enable us to be fully ourselves, and turn us into natural, unstrained activists, who give from overflow and a place of complete security.

In conclusion

There is a well-known prayer in the old Book of Common Prayer. It begins like this:

> O God, who art the author of peace
> And lover of concord,
> In knowledge of whom standeth
> Our eternal life,
> Whose service is perfect freedom...

None of us should have any difficulty in affirming the truth contained in the first four of these five lines. We might, however, struggle to agree with the fifth. Perhaps if it were to read, 'Whose service should be' or 'has the potential, at its best, to be ... perfect freedom ...', then that would be nearer the truth of our daily experience.

In Jesus, God has unquestionably done everything, from His side, that is necessary to give a person a life that is free. We became possessors of the keys to this freedom when we accepted Him as Lord.

That freedom has many ingredients, but it importantly includes:

- freedom from the need to earn love,
- freedom from the need to please,
- freedom to be ourselves,
- freedom from carrying other people's responsibilities,
- freedom from the need to control events and people,
- freedom to be spontaneous,
- freedom from sinful habits, and
- freedom from the guilt that accompanies them.

Possessing all these aspects of personal freedom depends on knowing God properly for ourselves. This means having an accurate and full grasp of who He is and what He is like, and of the fact of His unconditional and eternal love for us. More than knowing about God and His love in our heads, we must directly experience both in the depths of our being.

To do this requires nothing short of an inner revolution – a revolution that for many in the Body of Christ today has yet to take place.

Many of us are a long way from living in the perfect freedom that that old prayer describes. Instead captivity reigns within us. We are hemmed in and controlled by appetites and impulses that make slaves of us – by unforgiveness and sin conditions. Through these, we continue to try to meet needs which only God's (first healing, and then satisfying) love can ever properly meet. Through these, our relationships, our unity, our growth, our effectiveness, our peace, our security, our strength, our health, and our ability to give cheerfully continue to suffer. And through these, all the while, from deep down within us, the past still dictates our thinking and behaviour.

It is often said that 'time is a great healer'. The idea is that if we simply put time between ourselves and relationships or events that have damaged us, things will come right within us. Certainly there are situations where we benefit from time to cool down or to reflect. It is true, too, that time can cause the specifics of events and any pain associated with them to fade from our conscious senses, and so to lose much of their sting. But, as the real-life stories that we have related show, our inner wounds are never truly healed by the passage of time alone. Though we may forget them for long periods, they can remain, over decades, as fresh and powerful as they were when they were first inflicted upon us.

The truth is that God, and God alone, is the Great Healer. He can heal. He wants to heal. He waits only for His people to allow Him do so.